I WASN'T
ALWAYS
LIKE THIS

ESSAYS

SHELLEY A. LEEDAHL

Signature
EDITIONS

Cover design by Doowah Design.

Acknowledgements

This book was printed on Ancient Forest Friendly paper. Printed and bound in Canada by Hignell Book Printing Inc

We acknowledge the support of the Canada Council for the Arts and the Manitoba Arts Council for our publishing program.

Library and Archives Canada Cataloguing in Publication

Leedahl, Shelley A. (Shelley Ann), 1963-, author
    I wasn't always like this / Shelley A. Leedahl.

Issued in print and electronic formats.
ISBN 978-1-927426-51-7 (pbk.).--ISBN 978-1-927426-52-4 (epub)

    1. Leedahl, Shelley A. (Shelley Ann), 1963-. 2. Authors, Canadian (English)--20th century--Biography. I. Title.

PS8573.E3536Z473 2014   C813'.54   C2014-905383-5
                                       C2014-905384-3

Signature Editions
P.O. Box 206, RPO Corydon, Winnipeg, Manitoba, R3M 3S7
www.signature-editions.com

for

Florence Bevan

and in loving memory of my brother

Kirby Herr

～

1965–2012

CONTENTS

"How much I desire!
Inside my little satchel,
the moon, and flowers"

— Matsuo Bashō

ROAD TRIP

WE'RE ON HIGHWAY 16. MY HUSBAND'S DRIVING. THE kids are quiet and behaving in the back. The radio's playing "In the House of Stone and Light" — or "In the House of Stone and Love" — I can't quite make it out, but I like it. On this highway it's not hard to imagine why Columbus believed the world was flat; I feel we could drive right off the edge.

We're on our way to Meadow Lake, and I'm nervous about facing the hometown crowd. Will my old friends show? Will anyone? At Carpenter High — where I stumbled off the stage at my graduation and the principal came to my rescue — someone, perhaps the joker in the back row whose hair curls over his denim collar, will ask: *Why would anyone want to write about Saskatchewan?*

Because in another town, the town where I was born, the boy who lived above the meat market had two turtles, big as badgers, and we used to tear barefoot down the back alley over all the stones and it never hurt, it really never hurt, not like it did when I saw my first motorcycle, chased after it, then fell and sliced my knee so badly I still have the scar and there were plagues of grasshoppers on a white picket fence and Father fell off a roof and Sam Wong from Wong's Cafe on Main Street made milkshakes so thick you couldn't suck 'em up a straw and always, at night, the sound of soldiers, marching in my head.

I love this section of the highway. In the far right-hand corner of the sky: a breath of blue. *This is Saskatchewan*, they say. *Cold enough for you? Wet enough? Dry enough? Hot enough?* I can see the valley and the wide blue sash of the North Saskatchewan River. In summer, when everything's green as garden peas, this area reminds me of Scotland. Not that I've ever been there, but I've seen it often enough in movies to have a pretty good idea. My husband must have switched stations. "In the House of Stone and Light" (or "Love") is on again. Coming up to Borden. We pass the sign for Redberry Bible Camp.

Why write about Saskatchewan? Because at twelve I went to Starview Camp and all the girls had a crush on Counsellor Bob and we slept in sleeping bags beneath the stars and Thursday night at the campfire we were talking about religious stuff and this really weird thing happened...one camper started crying, then someone else and I thought, *It's not going to happen to me, whatever the hell it is*, and soon just about everyone was bawling and hugging each other—

even the guys—and I couldn't help it, my tears snuck up like a prairie storm and years later I saw Counsellor Bob in Saskatoon and met his wife, who was subbing at my kids' school, and no one ever talked about that night at the campfire again.

Why Saskatchewan? Because when I was twenty I crossed a picket line to work at the Westview Co-op on 33rd Street and my boyfriend had the best tan of his life walking that picket line and we had no idea I was pregnant 'cause I was on the Pill and that summer there was a major flood and I thought, *Oh, boy… God's pissed off now*, and everyone got to leave work early and I saw a Dickie Dee cart fall right over on its side like a big cow and the rain was coming down in walls and the treats spilled across the cement like manna and the Dickie Dee boy just stood there with the rain pinging off his head, he just stood there.

They're twinning the highway between Saskatoon and North Battleford. About time. Too many accidents. Phone lines: we hold our breath between them, see how many we can pass while humming one long note. Railroad tracks. That superstition: lift your feet for good luck. I lift mine now and will forever. Just past Maymont we pass a yellow school bus.

Why this place? Because that first snowfall each year makes you gasp, part of you glad that it's finally come after all the cold weather and wind and you know how happy all the little kids are because you can see them in the schoolyards sticking their tongues out for the candy of flakes, but there's that sinking feeling that this is the beginning of it, this is the long haul, the lugging out of boots and pairing of gloves, the frosted windshields and battery cables...Why write about this? Here?

Because I remember watching that first snowfall from a friend's bedroom window. She lived in the country. We took the bus. It had a funny name—Clover Bell, or something. Loads of kids in her family and it was loud in her house but there, by the window, just then, it was quiet and the snow was confetti and I would never have guessed that years later I would read that this friend died in a freak accident— electrocuted while vacuuming her van—and I heard her mother was going to raise her son and I was sorry for it all, the orphaned little boy, the grieving mother, and my friend, who never knew what it meant to me, that first snowfall through her bedroom window.

54-40. "Ocean Pearl." I like this song. The landscape has no colour now, but it's a sly chameleon, this prairie. In a few months, another season and a new palette. New textures, too. Coarse crops. Powdery dust. And those big fat cumulus clouds we imagine into sheep and fellow animals. Speaking of, there is a pasture alive with horses, not knowing they are beautiful.

Why write? Because I had the fourteen-year-old's fling with horses—Prince, Candy, Black—and was lucky to have friends who owned them. That summer at Lorene's when we were all riding bareback, then we met up with the boys and we were swinging our legs over the edge of knowing and night and never looking back and we saw that UFO and we were all pinned there, beneath a white, blipping light that two-stepped around the stars and likely no one believes us but we were there and as sure as a cocktail of dirt and manure was caked beneath our runners there was an unidentified object, flying.

Now we're on the oldies station. "Hot Child in the City." I remember when this song came out. Nick Gilder. Trooper. Supertramp. My God: *I'm* an oldie! My husband, T, hasn't spoken for several minutes. We get like this on road trips. The sign for the Denholm Hotel says Rooms. T blurts, "There's the sun," like it's a long-lost friend, and it is. It's also still snowing. Pools of water sit like flattened sapphires upon the still-blank faces of fields. Give it a few days. Saskatchewan is the sunshine capital of North America.

Why? Because we are children of the sun and I will never regret my teenage years, all those nights at the lake, on the lake, in it. I don't regret the parties, the concerts, the trips to the neon cities that were another world I was desperate to explore, knew it from the time I was a little kid and my father took us to Saskatoon. It used to wake the butterflies in my stomach when I saw the first grey outline of skyscrapers, or better, the thin long line of lights in the night that spelled a word on the tip of my tongue.

Why would anyone want to write about Saskatchewan? Because of the boy with pet turtles and my friend of the first snowfall. Because of the sun and the coldest damn rinks you could imagine. Because I've never been to Scotland. Because, as the song goes: "I can see for miles and miles." Because of thick vanilla milkshakes in metal containers at Wong's Cafe, Main Street, Kyle, Saskatchewan. Because of the ghosts of elevators that are fondly remembered dreams and the wheat-like stalks that are power poles. Because in Lucky Lake, everyone still says hello to strangers. Because there's a lighthouse on a hill in Cochin, where few ships ever come in. Because of haunted houses and hollyhocks. Because all across this province there are cemeteries, and beside them, there were drive-in theatres, and on Sunday nights kids lined up for hours for the triple feature. They snuck beer in, and maybe a friend or two in the trunk, and when I was a little kid, Dad took me to *Tales from the Crypt* at the drive-in beside the cemetery where Grandma was sleeping and it scared and scarred me for life.

Because I was born here. Learned to read and write here. Caught my first butterfly here. My first fish. Chicken pox. This is where I learned to do the one-foot-spin and played spin the bottle. Because of the sunsets and skyscrapers, small-town parades and fathers who are Kinsmen and Elks. Because of riverbanks, ball diamonds, and beaches.

Because there are still almost a million people here whose stories deserve to be told and most will never put pen to paper. Because around here we weave through good times and bad, through love and desire, just like everyone anywhere else. We stumble, dust ourselves off, and get back on the trail.

Because of all of these things but, especially, because some day someone might want to know what it was like to live in this particular part of the country, the world, the universe, at this particular point in time, and I want to be able to say, *Listen, it was like this.*

NO OCEAN, NO MOUNTAINS

THERE'S NO PLACE LIKE HOME

THE DOG SMELLS A DEPARTURE, FEARS HIS EXCLUSION. This is no ordinary 5:00 a.m.: the children are up and helping us load the minivan with everything we deem necessary for our five-week cross-Canada quest. We've journeyed west many times; now our collective sights are set on the east. This is the "Newfoundland or Bust" tour, and Cape Spear is as far east as she gets, B'y.

Inventory:

Tennis racquets?

Check.

Crossword puzzles?

Yep.

Lucy Maude Montgomery novels?

Uh huh.

Camp stove?

Whoops—good catch.

The children think it's about landscape and capitals, history and geography, and it is. But it's also about stitching together what unravels throughout the year: the delicate threads of a family relationship. I want to know my son and daughter, really *know* them, apart from the glimpses I get of their T-shirts as they wing out the door with friends. I want them to be each other's best friend, if only for the next few weeks. I'll ask strangers to take our photo while we eat ice cream cones at the Halifax harbour, or do cartwheels on the Plains of Abraham. I'm banking on some MasterCard moments: priceless.

Of course it's not *all* about the kids—I also want to see Winnipeg, Montreal and Cornerbook through my husband's eyes, as well as my own—but our progeny are the major impetus. Like all well-meaning parents, we want the best educations possible for our children, and figure our bit includes introducing them to as much of this great country as we can financially manage. We'd experience each province as soon as they were old enough to appreciate it and still young enough to want to be seen with us. The clock is ticking: Logan is fourteen. Next year he'll have a summer job, a learner's licence, a girlfriend. Taylor, twelve, has gone into premature mourning over the separation from best friends, Jaime and Dylan. I expect she'll survive.

There's also the literary mileage (and tax write-offs) implicit in a trip like this. I'll change names and locations, blur facts, spice up the drama. My short story will be fabricated, *mais oui*, but it'll ride neck-and-neck down the highway with fact.

It's now 6:04 a.m., and the Ford Aerostar's packed. There's just enough room for bodies between two tents, a glut of camping gear, food, bikes, and four clothes-crammed hockey bags. We've got maps, CAA campground books, an itinerary scrawled on the back of one of my poetic miscues, five weeks of freedom, and eight eyes pegged on the rising sun. T turns the engine over: an unnatural ticking shatters the dawn. Some things have been left to fate, or faith.

My mother-in-law, she of the CAA membership (for which we are grateful and well-stocked in maps), cries as she is wont, and clutches the whimpering dog by his self-chewed collar. She is house-sitter and pet-sitter: we cannot leave the house alone, not in this neighbourhood, not in this century.

I crave the unknown and the highway, though my first desire is for sleep. Last night, anticipation brewing, I managed a brief forty-five minutes. Saskatchewan, I think, is for sleeping. With husband at the wheel, maps creased on my lap and the kids buckled into the back, we hit College Drive just as the sun crests above the greystone buildings on campus. *An adventure a day* is our mantra.

∼

Why Don't You Sing?

No one had said anything for a long time, then Clark turned the radio off and hitched his shoulders: left, right, left again. He did a little shifting in his seat and fiddled with the air conditioner. It made a sound like an electric weed snipper. "Jesus," he said, running two fingers beneath his collar.

Kit saw that something was eating him. He scratched his forearm and left four white trails on his skin; they'd forgotten the nail-clippers. *Her* fault.

"We're taking a chance, Kit. You know that." He kept his eyes on the eighteen-wheeler ahead, wondering where it might be headed, and if that driver had covered as much of the map of Canada as they already had. He doubted it.

"Mm." Kit *did* know they were taking a chance, but she'd been busy watching the landscape change after they'd left Ottawa, a city with a lot going for it, she decided, and her concern was temporarily diminished. In the nation's capital they'd witnessed "The Changing of the Guard" and toured the Parliament Buildings, grateful for refuge from the searing sun. Before their bubbly—she'd actually laughed *too* much, Kit thought—college-aged guide began leading them through the maze of cool interior rooms, the girl listed each province east to west to discover where her charge of tourists hailed from. Cheers and applause erupted when people and provinces matched.

Kit wasn't surprised that they were the sole Albertans. "Lethbridge," she said, voluntarily. "South of Calgary." Twenty people turned to gawk, as if Kit and kin were aliens. A moment of respectful silence followed, then the guide tittered and the gang of geographically diverse Canadians and a lone male from Pittsburgh gave an extra loud whoop. So this is Ottawa, Kit thought.

The family'd poked their noses into floral bouquets at the Byward Market and watched houseboats and speedboats rise up the lock. Women pranced on decks in bikini tops and wrap-around mini-skirts. They gripped tall drinks, and Clark said they resembled actors in a commercial for the good life. The Albertans hadn't time for the National Gallery or the Supreme Court of Canada, but they glimpsed the Rideau Canal and 24 Sussex Drive: not a Chrétien in sight.

Kit was embracing the distractions, and trying not to dwell on what she'd committed her beloveds to. She thought about reassuring Clark once again. She could profess: "Listen, we're still fairly young and adventurous, and we wanted to see Quebec while it's still part of the country. Besides, who else do we know there?" But she was too exhausted for the weight of all those words, and not sure she believed them anyway—especially the bit about both of them being adventurous. She had to push Clark into almost everything: vacations, knock-off Birkenstock sandals, Uncle Ben's Assorted Wild Rice, other people. "We sure laughed with those Frenchies, eh?"

Clark eased. "Yeah," he said, clicking the radio on again. A Top 40 pop song about wanting the highway was playing—their summer theme song. Everyone sang along except Clark: in their sixteen years of marriage he'd never once sung out loud. "Laurent was a funny guy."

"Hilarious."

But they hardly knew the man, Clark realized, and he hadn't a hot clue as to what kind of trouble might greet them at the end of this tedious day. They'd spent two hours with Laurent and his girlfriend, Isabel, at a four-star Cuban resort a year and a half earlier. Clark and Kit's first major holiday. A little hallelujah before their accountant's counsel on the benefits of declaring bankruptcy.

Kit adjusted her bargain store sunglasses: they were causing a welt behind her left ear. "Remember that thing about the diarrhoea and not being able to flush the toilet?"

"Yeah." Clark checked the rearview mirror to be sure he had a good jump on the semi before he careened back into the right lane. The speed of everything out here gave him hives. In Lethbridge only the wind moved this fast. "Laurent pretended to squirt out a sundae, complete with sound effects. He killed me."

He was driving like a woman, Kit noted, hands on the wheel in the ten-and-two position. The kids always bugged her about driving like an old lady. "How you two doing back there?"

Jordy grunted. "We're packed in here like sardines," he said, flinging a tanned arm out from behind his sister's back, "but we're loving every minute of it. Yay Canada!" At fourteen he was still mostly a child, and Kit revelled in his enthusiasm for innocent activities like catching frogs and throwing Frisbees. If a tree was climbable, he'd scramble up. If a stone could be skipped, he'd out-skip them all.

His sister was two years younger and exactly the same height; they were often mistaken for twins. Chantal had oozed confidence since she was fully potty-trained at eighteen months. She now broke into a screaming version of the national anthem. She was in a children's choir that sang with the symphony. She was vice-president of her elementary school. She won red ribbons in track meets. And she possessed a tongue like a whip.

"Chantal, can it!" Jordy ordered.

The girl held one more long note, then said, "I've lost the feeling in my legs."

"Move the sleeping bags," Clark suggested. "Throw something else on the floor." He was trying. Like the Varadero vacation, this whole cross-Canada thing had been Kit's idea. He guessed that the children would prefer *not* to be squashed into the minivan for multiple weeks, their dirty bare feet resting on cases of Alberta-brewed beer intended for eastern Canadians—or if the going got rough enough, for driver and co-pilot. He would have been happy with their usual two weeks at his parents' condo in Kelowna, but Kit had other ideas. Kit *always* had other ideas.

"The kids are growing up," she'd said. "It's time we saw this country of ours."

"So we'll get a coffee-table book," he'd said. "I think Mom has—"

"Clark, I mean it. We're doing this."

And so on July 3rd, morning not yet broken, their sensible neighbours still dreams away from waking, they backed out of their driveway while Kit's mother gripped the collar of their desperate Irish wolfhound—another of Kit's inspirations, but no one was sorry. Clark thought the dog on its hind legs—paws clawing the air—resembled Dick Van Dyke.

"He knows this is gonna be a long one," Jordy'd said, craning his neck out the window until dog, grandmother and even Lethbridge were out of sight.

"Stop squirming!" Ever impassioned, Chantal was the child who came home with report card comments about disrupting the class. Clark thought she would become a feminist lawyer. Kit had slapped her once. Chantal slapped right back, but harder. "Jordy, you're drooling again. Move over! Mom, did you drop Jordy on his head when he was a baby?" She squealed. "Mom, he pinched me!"

Kit sighed. "Settle down, you two...there's room for both of you." Those damn bikes. She pitched a dark look at Clark. They'd quarrelled about the bikes; even dismantled they took up a great deal of space. She'd wanted to leave them, he insisted they come; they hadn't used them yet.

Clark prided himself on his van-packing abilities. He dreamt about different configurations. He thought about how he'd managed it all this time: two tents, four lawn chairs, a basket of shoes, their clothes crammed into four hockey bags with failing zippers, tennis racquets, a camp stove, tarps, ropes, an axe and a hatchet, two single sleeping foams and one double, the Coleman cooler they'd received as a wedding gift, a lantern, flashlights, a large box of cookware and utensils, laundry detergent, the perpetually full dirty clothes' bag, firewood (grabbed free wherever possible), two plastic containers of non-perishable groceries, bike helmets and the two disassembled bikes (two more on the bike rack, which had to come off each time they needed to open the van's back door); this was their situation.

The children shared their space with pillows, sleeping bags, knapsacks and whatever paraphernalia they'd brought along to lessen the boredom of ten- to twelve-hour driving days. Chantal was on a Lucy Maude Montgomery kick; they'd be camping at Cavendish, Prince Edward Island, and visiting the Anne of Green Gables house.

Jordy'd brought handheld video games that buzzed and beeped and made Kit want to kick out a window. He'd also smuggled in sunflower seeds.

The kids knew they weren't supposed to eat the seeds in the van, but as Chantal professed, neither of them expected Canada to be so freaking big.

Kit agreed. It was one thing to see your country on a map and scoot your finger between the borders, quite another to drive and camp across its girth.

East of Manitoba the country became one giant forest. She broke down on the north shore of Lake Superior. "Eat your bloody spits, then. But don't you dare spill pop on the seats!"

Jordy and Chantal each had a journal for recording impressions about this "once-in-a-lifetime trip." Kit was certain they were deliberately losing pens and misplacing the journals, and by the third week she caved on this, too. They'd always have the photos.

~

Two and a half hours of driving and we're much further than we thought we'd be. Now we're passing the town where I was invited to read the story "Spades" from my 1994 collection *Sky Kickers* at the local high school, then *un*invited when someone—a teacher? the principal? a parent?—had concerns about its suitability. Elements of the occult? That certainly wouldn't do, and the gig was called off. (This is my life.) That $200 would have bought reams of paper and stamps.

By Saltcoats we're still making excellent time. T says: *This is serious Mennonite country.*

Logan: *Are those the people you can kick and they won't fight back?*

I'm trying not to pee until we hit Manitoba. The distance will be a record for me, but I think I can, I think I can.

In Churchbridge we whiz past the world's largest one-dollar coin. We missed seeing the "world's longest bike" near Langenburg.

We leave Saskatchewan in the proverbial and literal dust at 10:14 a.m.. Yahoo: potty break.

~

With each new border Clark knew more about the science of keeping food cool—if not frozen—with bags of fast-melting ice. He judged a city by the price of two things: gas and five-pound bags of ice. He'd learned that you need to hit the campgrounds before supper; that the harder a campground was to find the better it would be. They followed a faded sign near Spanish, Ontario and drove through tracks in a field to discover a rustic fishing resort. Two serene lakes were connected by waterfalls worthy of *Canadian Geographic*. They camped on the shore beneath a canopy of fragrant poplars, leaves tinkling in the breeze like tinfoil hung in a garden to discourage crows. The kids fished off a bridge and caught and released eighty pan fish; even Clark had to admit that this was one place he'd return to.

Kit was learning, too. She learned that washing a muddy tent in a laundromat made one hell of a mess; the reason no one took that nice site in the campground at

Lake Winnipeg's Grand Beach was because of the red ants; she'd always have to be the first to start tearing down camp in the morning so they could get on the road again; and if she drank anything after 8:00 p.m. she'd have to get up in the dead of night to pee behind the tent. Also, warm juice on a hot day was better than no juice at all.

"We're going to lose the sun," Clark was saying. "How much further's Montreal?"

Kit had two maps unfolded on her lap—a map of Montreal and an Ontario-Quebec combo. She also had a CAA guide to campgrounds and their itinerary—typed on yellow paper for easy identification—sticking to her legs. Simultaneously following the lines on the maps, calculating distances and reading the CAA book made her nauseous, but she didn't complain any longer. When she had, Clark threatened to stop the van and make her drive, so he could take "the easy job."

Then one of the kids would yell: "Stop fighting!"

"We should be there in about forty-five," she said. "Less than an hour." Their quandary resurfaced as a tightness in her throat: two thumbs exerting a gentle but increasing pressure on her larynx. She took another sip of pop; the choker-collar remained. Maybe Laurent wouldn't even show, though three weeks earlier, on the phone, he'd sounded certain.

"Hello Bay-bee," he'd crooned.

She'd forgotten the accent: thick as maple syrup, dripping with innuendo.

"I'm so glad you remember me," she'd said. "Remember *us*. Me. And Clark. Clark and I." Oh, mercy.

And then it flew back: how he'd openly appraised her floral sundress; how he'd actually asked to squeeze her calf muscles; his delight in her hearty laugh (that made the Swedes at the next table scowl). The humidity had done good things to her hair, and he played his fingers through it, innocently enough—apropos of a conversation about how chlorine dries one's hair to a crisp.

She'd felt all right beneath that Cuban sun. Like someone else. It was all good.

"He said 8:30, right? At the Orange Julep on Decarie Boulevard." Clark could feel his shoulders stiffening. He could relate to a jack-in-the-box.

"Yes. It's supposed to be very easy to find," she said. "A huge orange. He said he'd be waiting." She goosed her neck to look at the kids; quick turns made her feel sick, too. The kids were dozing again. Chantal's head had fallen onto Jordy's lap, her hair a fine blonde web across his knees. She couldn't imagine how that would be comfortable, but the pair had intermittently snoozed in yoga-like positions through the last three provinces. A bubble of Jordy's saliva was beginning its slow descent. How sweet they were. And vulnerable. "Honey, are we crazy?"

Clark patted her thigh. She'd often noted that his beefy hands were the only part of him that stored any extra fat. People stared at his fingers. Kit's best friend said she'd seen smaller penises. "We'll soon find out."

~

Minnedosa, Manitoba is set in a green valley; it's simply charming.

Taylor's a little hyper but the kids are generally travelling well. I read my journal entry out loud to them. So they know.

In Neepawa, mother and daughter visit Margaret Laurence's childhood home. Only $2, and a guided tour to boot. This is where Laurence set *A Bird in the House*. I see the typewriter she used. I use her toilet and wash my hands in the original sink. A sign in the bathroom states: *The towel is for display only. Please use the paper towel provided.* I use the towel; maybe a little Margaret will rub off.

I take two outdoor pictures: my flash is kaput and thus I've left it at home. A dozen or so seniors are listening to a lecture in the sunny yard. Elderhostel. I can't wait until I can do elderhostels.

I am here and not here. I could spend hours in this house, absorbing, but T and Logan will soon be back with the gas tank replenished, and we still have a long drive to our first destination: Grand Beach, Lake Winnipeg, where I've reserved a campsite. I expect I'll be glad of the foresight: I've heard that Grand Beach is rated among the top ten beaches in the world. It will be just what I need—soft white sand and a swim at the end of the highway.

~

Everything had been different in Varadero. The sun moved jauntily across the sky, birds were friendlier. She'd only seen palm trees on-screen before Cuba. The days were patternless. So this is how the other half live, she'd thought. I could do this. I could fit. She resented not being able to talk Clark onto a motorbike—so they could see more of the island—but that was her single regret.

They'd met Laurent and Isabel beside the pool, where a trio of Cubans performed American love songs from the 1970s. "You don't mind us joining you?" Kit had said, already sliding a chair out to sit at the patio table. Clark had wanted to leave. There was a mini-mall across the boulevard where they could order pizza by the slice, or grilled chicken. No waiting in a buffet queue, no talking to strangers.

"Please." Laurent swept a brown arm across the turquoise placemats and napkins—sea shades, Kit noted—and smiled broadly. The short sleeves of his white rayon shirt had been rolled up and pressed back. "Our pleasure."

She'd seen him earlier in the week. His was the kind of face one noticed, she thought: angular, with wide brown eyes, a handsome scar on his chin. Slash with a hockey stick? Bar fight? His long hair was scooped neatly into a ponytail, and he sported a well-kept goatee. He wore a brief red bathing suit around the pool, and possessed the broad shoulders and wide ribcage of a swimmer. But he was smaller than most men, she noted. Much too tiny for someone like herself. He couldn't have been more different than her tall, solid husband. Clark's sandy hair was clipped respectably above his ears, and she was proud of the fact that his build suggested *firefighter*, or *cop*. Congenial Clark, whom everyone liked but few got close to, was a high school phys-ed teacher. He coached basketball and shot hoops himself every Wednesday night. She felt safe with him—on the streets of Havana, in the forests of Canada. He was her *type*.

"Are you Canadians?" she'd asked, sitting across from Laurent. At eye level.

"Yes, from Montreal. And you?"

"Lethbridge, Alberta."

His eyes brightened, and she saw how his smile transformed his face. He had small teeth: even, and white as—she thought for a moment—white as antelope bones in a ditch.

Isabel was pretty in the European sense, Kit thought, with short dark hair that emphasized large eyes and shapely cheekbones. She reminded Kit of Juliette Binoche, who'd played both the nurse in *The English Patient* and the sizzling sex-a-holic in *Damage* (which she'd seen seven times and highly recommended) alongside Jeremy Irons. Kit adored Jeremy Irons. She was fond of saying no one played obsession better.

Isabel frequently stumbled with her English. She'd turn to Laurent for help, and he'd whip a few firecrackers back at her. Kit noticed that he finished everything his wife began.

"To Canada," Laurent said, touching his wine glass to Clark's bottle of Cristal beer, "and new friends."

They drank, ate, drank more, and conversation deteriorated into nonsense.

Laurent punctuated observations about other tourists and hotel staff with sound effects and grand gesticulations. He made cracks about ninety-year-old Danes falling out of G-strings. Juvenile or not, everything made them howl. The Swedes left en masse.

"He was a big talker," Clark said, setting the cruise control up a notch. "Bragged about his toys. I wonder how much of it was true. Maybe they're struggling—"

"Like us," Kit finished. Before they'd left, Clark's father'd insisted that they had "no bloody business gallivanting to all corners" when they couldn't even afford to get their fridge working properly. Their van, he bet, would strand them in Gander or Lunenberg. *Then* what?

It was more of a slam against Kit. Her bookstore in the strip mall had gone under after Varadero; they'd lost everything they'd invested, and then some. There were no RRSPs, no college funds for the children, and they'd had to remortgage the house. Now she was painting landscapes. A life-long passion, but Clark's father thought it ludicrous. Kit was not swayed. Shingles peeled, the van made mysterious noises, clothes were second-hand: it didn't matter. Seeing Canada was a priority. "Where there's a will..." And she knew how to travel cheaply. She'd written notes to everyone they knew east of Alberta and warned them they'd be coming. Could they pitch a tent in the backyard? Only two parties responded: a great-aunt of Clark's in Truro, Nova Scotia—who'd raised chinchillas before her hip replacement—and Laurent.

That distant night by the pool—which officially closed at six—Laurent'd coaxed Clark into a midnight dip. It was so unlike Clark, breaking the rules, cavorting in wet boxers before beautiful strangers. Having big fun. They'd swapped phone numbers and addresses; Laurent and Isabel had to fly home the next day.

Back in their hotel room—with the rattan furniture and sandy floor—Kit told Clark that she thought Isabel was stunning. "Very few women can pull off short hair."

"Sure, she's beautiful," he'd said, "but *you're* different."

Kit felt her cheeks warm. It was as close to a compliment as she ever got.

~

Near Winnipeg, about forty minutes from Grand Beach now, and it's only 4:00 p.m. Manitoba time. We skirt the edge of the city, plow through a grey wall of rain—cloudburst, as it turns out; the kids stick their heads out the windows and get soaked—and are soon back on the sunny side of the hour. Temperature: 29 degrees, and breezeless.

~

They'd found the Orange Julep—unmissable, as Laurent had promised—but nowhere in the parking lot did they see the blue Mercedes he'd told them to look for. The sun was dropping behind the giant orange but the evening remained warm. After tangy juleps they returned to the canteen for ice water. Clark asked a grizzled old-timer where the washrooms were; directions flew back in French.

"So where's the nearest campground?" Jordy snapped the CAA book from Kit's hands.

"We might have to drive to Drummondville," Kit said. "I don't think your father'd be too keen on pitching the tents in the middle of Montreal."

"Drummondville!" Clark had changed into pants in the bathroom. His good ones. "Isn't that halfway to Quebec City?" He was beat, and Kit was wrong. He told her he would have been happy to throw beach towels over the windows and sleep right there, in the Orange Julep parking lot in the heart of Montreal. Laurent be damned!

They'd been waiting thirty-five minutes. Kit was about ready to give up, too.

"Wait!" Chantal leaned through the seats. "Is that a Mercedes?"

Kit stepped out of the van. "Oh, my God, I think that's him."

Laurent honked twice before he eased the car in beside them. "My friends!" His gold watch flashed as he opened his arms to welcome first Clark, then Kit, who flushed when she received his two-cheek kiss. *"Bienvenue!* Isabel is at the house. Kit, you come with me … Clark can follow."

Kit glanced at Clark as if to communicate: *I didn't plan this. I'm as freaked as you are, and no, I won't do anything to jeopardize our sixteen years of wedded bliss … well … mostly bliss.* Soon she was climbing into the Mercedes' creamy interior. "I can't believe we're actually here. I bet you thought you'd never see us again, eh?"

They'd stopped at a red light. Clark was two cars behind, and in the wrong lane. She crossed her fingers for him.

"It's good to have you. We've been looking forward to it." He smiled. At her. She pushed her hair—a sophisticated, shoulder-length cut, not long and loose as it had been in Cuba—behind her ear and stared ahead.

They made their way out of the city, into the hilly countryside, where palatial new houses with swimming pools and trampolines defined a landscape of privilege and fun.

"I work there." Laurent pointed to a flat, stuccoed building. Kit tried to recall what he did for a living. Jewellery sales? Jewellery repair? Jewellery theft? The nondescript building offered up no clues.

They drove a long time. Her frequent checks verified that Clark was right behind them, hunched over the steering wheel but holding his own. Jordy had taken her seat in front.

"Isabel will be so happy to see you. We're having a baby."

"That's wonderful!" She touched his arm, as she often did to people when surprised. She hoped he wouldn't take it the wrong way. Surely he wouldn't; they were demonstrative people, these Québécois. Always touching and kissing, and Laurent had affectionately called Clark *brother*.

It was dusk now, which increased her disorientation. They were on a lane nearing a sprawling brick home.

Clark coasted in behind the Mercedes. The van was embarrassingly loud—something, somewhere, was not right—and he hoped Laurent hadn't noticed. "Here we are," Clark said, and turned off the key, but Jordy and Chantal were already out the doors.

A Jeep Grand Cherokee gleamed beside the Benz. Clark spotted a speedboat, a motorcycle, his and hers snowmobiles. *Shucks*, he thought.

Pink geraniums led up a flagstone driveway lit with ornate lanterns on gothic, wrought-iron poles. The expansive coach house featured a multi-tiered deck and white-pillared entrance. Two bronze lions flanked either side of the red double doors. Chantal patted a lion head and whispered in Kit's ear: "Are these guys rich or what?"

"It's—" Kit caught her breath, "—lovely."

The front door opened and Isabel stepped out. "*Allô!*" She too, welcomed them with wide arms and butterfly kisses. "You are looking so good!"

"Congratulations," Kit said, smelling Isabel's perfume, "on the baby. Are you feeling okay?"

"*Ah, oui.* Better now. At first—" She gripped her throat and shook her head.

Inside, Kit set her University of Calgary backpack on the Italian marble floor. Clearly, this was a house where no children kicked off shoes, flopped on the couch, or dragged supper from the table to eat in front of the TV. Floors shone, furniture matched, the kitchen was a white-on-white metaphor for cleanliness. She found herself holding her breath.

Isabel spoke in French, then turned to Kit with an apology: "Forgive me. I'm trying to learn English, but it's not easy for me."

Laurent jumped in. "She asked me to show the kids the pool. We'll eat in the pool house, and the kids can sleep there tonight."

Jordy looked at Chantal. The girl clapped her hands to her face and beamed. Kit saw that the blue polish on her daughter's fingernails was half chipped off. She guessed Jordy hadn't combed his hair in days.

"You have bathing suits?" Laurent asked.

"We can get them," Jordy said, and pushed his bangs from his eyes.

"We'll sleep in there, too, if that's okay." Clark still wasn't sure if he could trust this guy as far as he could throw him, good time in Cuba or not.

Laurent pouted and looked up at the taller man. "But we have the guest room made up for you. It'd be nice to sleep on a bed, no? Have a little privacy?" He jerked his head toward the children.

Kit grinned. Her kids were old enough to understand the innuendo, but she still doubted if they believed she and Clark had sex; they'd discovered some *very* quiet methods. "Thanks, it would be, but Clark's right. We'll just put our foams and sleeping bags in the pool house now. Jords, you can bring that stuff from the van, right?"

The boy said he could, and the Albertans followed their host outside to inspect the large rectangular pool. Kit took it all in. An inflatable recliner bobbed on the water, and the deck was large enough for twin chaise lounges, side tables, and six blue ceramic pots with trailing orange and red nasturtiums. It smelled just like Cuba, she thought. That combination of sunshine and flowers. She would never know luxuries like these. The kids dipped their hands into the sparkling water. "Cool!" they said in unison.

"Get your suits then," Clark said, and he and Kit followed Laurent back into the house.

The host cracked ice into glasses at the sideboard. "Scotch okay?"

"Sure," Clark said. "Love one." He'd never had Scotch in his life. As a rule, hard liquor gave him chest pains. Would his hospitalization card be valid in Quebec, he wondered?

He looked for a place to sit. The leather couch was the colour of desert sand. It looked terribly soft. He might have a hell of a time getting out of it.

"I'll pass for now," Kit said, before Laurent had time to offer her a drink. "We brought you something. I'll be right back." She jogged out to the Aerostar, where Chantal was already struggling into her bikini beneath the cover of a beach towel.

"Isn't this awesome?" the girl said.

"Yeah. You guys better behave. I don't think these people are used to having kids around. No splashing or drowning each other. Hear me?"

Kit extricated one of the cases of Big Rock and returned to the house. Clark was now alone in the front room. He had finished most of his drink, she noticed, and his shoulders were relaxed. He seemed happier now that he was no longer behind the wheel and had the promise of food ahead. It was almost 10:00 p.m.; in Alberta they ate at 5:30. Soon she heard Jordy and Chantal making an unholy ruckus in the outdoor pool. "We're eating in the pool house," Clark said. Isabel appeared from the kitchen with a plate of heaped nachos. Laurent was cradling a bowl of three-bean salad.

Kit and Clark followed their friends into the octagonal pool house, windows on all sides. "This is amazing," she said, and another wave of envy lapped across her.

"So, my crazy brother," Laurent said, tapping Clark's shoulder, "you're going to Newfoundland?"

"Newfoundland or bust. We're travelling as far east as one possibly can on this continent. Hope to see a whale or two, maybe tour a lighthouse, then we'll turn around and head back. Damn well better be worth it."

Isabel asked Kit: "How is your trip so far?"

"Really great," Kit answered. "It was rather long driving across some parts of Ontario, and we got a little screwed up in Thunder Bay, but overall it's been good. We love Quebec."

The kids were mummied in towels and standing at the patio doors, waiting for permission to enter. Kit waved them in, embarrassed at how they attacked the food.

"This is great," Jordy said, spitting nacho crumbs. He wiped salsa off his chin, then raced Chantal back to the pool. "Last one in's a—"

Laurent lit a cigarette and Kit watched the smoke arabesque toward the ceiling fan. "So where you two going this winter?" he asked. "Jamaica? Barbados?"

Kit caught Clark in a wince. "We...we haven't decided yet." They weren't going anywhere, not for a long time, she knew. After this, they would cut up the credit cards. They'd shred them. Or burn them. Or bury them in the four corners of the yard.

Isabel sprang up. "Oh—*merde*, I almost forgot." She reached toward the CD player above the bar. She wasn't showing much yet, Kit noticed. The music was loud, tropical, and familiar.

Kit said, "I don't believe it."

Isabel touched her shoulder: a quick, friendly gesture. The pregnant woman looked pleased.

"What's this?" Clark turned, as if having his ear face the CD player would help him distinguish the music.

"You don't remember?" Laurent pursed his lips. "You're getting old, my friend!"

"It's…is it the music from our trip?" Clark leaned forward.

"This is that song they kept playing at the hotel bar, remember?" Kit began singing, *"Besos y nada más…"*

Isabel was swaying, then Laurent pulled Kit off her chair and their hips found the Latin beat. Soon all three were singing the chorus.

"What the hell." Clark set down his drink and began his own unique dance. He made little chest-level punches in the air, as if shaking maracas.

"Come on, Clark, you know the words," Kit teased. She knew he wouldn't sing. He went through his whole life mouthing songs—hymns, "Farewell to Nova Scotia," whatever was played on the radio—but no lyrics crossed his lips. It was an enigma. She could understand when they'd first started going out and were shy with each other, but now, after all these years? There was nothing left to hide. She'd asked him once, "Why don't you sing?" He'd answered with something flip, like, "Why don't you drive race cars or shave your head bald?"

The music pulsed. They moved the table to make more room. Kit was really shaking it. She'd watched the Cuban women dance—back, step, up, up, back, step—and imitated her memory of them, even doing the "washing machine," a one-foot pivot and medium-slow twirl while her pelvis shook in triple-time.

Laurent thrust out a knee. Isabel lifted her already short dress and rode his leg while their hips rotated. So sexy, Kit thought.

On the other side of the glass, Jordy heaved himself out of the deep end and wiped water from his eyes. "Hey, Chantal...check it out."

Chantal stood on the deck and dripped. Her father had grabbed Isabel's hips, Isabel had Laurent's, and ew, Laurent had his hands on their mother while they snaked around the room, tossing their heads and cawing. "How many provinces left?"

"Four," Jordy said flatly. "Eleven if you count going back."

The patio doors slid open. Music spilled across the pool and into the surrounding pines. The adults conga-lined around the deck. Clark pulled off his T-shirt and whipped it over his shoulder. It landed in a yellow rose bush.

"Dad, what are you doing?" Jordy jumped off the pool deck. If his father was going to make a complete fool of himself, he preferred not to be a witness.

Isabel started clapping while Clark unzipped his pants and slid them over his thighs. Only then did Kit, on the end of the line, see what was happening. Her right arm shot up as if to stop Clark from going any further, but he got his size 13 feet out of his pants and dove—deeply, brilliantly—into the moonlit water.

He came up spouting blood.

"Clark!" Kit reached with both arms and lurched toward the water.

Clark touched his mouth, gawked at his dark fingertips. "It's just a little cut. I must have bitten my lip when I hit the bottom." His head was throbbing. He thought he might black out.

Laurent charged into the pool house and returned with ice cubes. Kit held them to the back of Clark's neck. Isabel and the children stood on the sidelines like effigies. The music played on.

"*Mon Dieu*, you've chipped three teeth!" Isabel cried.

～

The site I'd reserved at Grand Beach (Bay 15, #8) is truly lousy, so we've moved to Bay 15, #3. Now T is being repeatedly bitten by red ants, mosquitoes and horseflies as he struggles to erect the tent. The kids and I grind the ferocious ants into the dirt with a heel-stomp, step-spin action. It becomes a bizarre game, a funky dance. We laugh a lot, and I offer that old adage: *If it weren't for bad luck, we wouldn't have any.*

First lesson: never set up camp until *after* we've inspected the site.

We warm up canned stew and soup…just before the camp stove quits. T fiddles with it, and frustration mounts. Still no action. He makes a funnel out of paper. It leaks. We have driven all day; no one needs this.

Finally, we leave for the beach. There are very few people here. A mother and her two daughters on the sand. Some teenaged parents with their toddler. A few other young people splashing in the water and shouting obscenities, jeans rolled to their knees. The bellies of small fish flash silver as dimes. The sun is setting, the water is calm and clear as far as we can see.

Firewood is $4.50 a bundle; we all gather driftwood and haul it back to the campsite. Ha! And they thought they'd make us buy wood.

~

"I'm so tired I could puke," Clark said. They'd spread the foams and sleeping bags across the pool-house floor. Outside, the water shimmered black and gold.

"Did you set your watch alarm?" Kit asked him.

"Yes."

"We've got to be up by six. Laurent leaves for work at seven."

"I said I did already."

"Fine."

And they slept, shoulder to shoulder to shoulder to shoulder, the children book-ended on either side.

Kit heard the alarm first. "Get up, everyone. It's five after six."

Jordy groaned. Clark rolled.

Chantal sniffed and asked: "What's that disgusting smell?'

"What smell?" Kit was popping her contacts in. She could take it if Laurent or Isabel saw her with morning hair, but her glasses were another matter. The frames themselves—a rather generic, oval shape that had worked from 1985 until now—weren't the problem. She was extremely nearsighted, and when she'd purchased the glasses she hadn't splurged on the expensive lenses which reduced thickness. Her lenses exceeded their frames by a healthy quarter inch. "I said, 'what smell?'"

"That pee smell."

Clark was sitting now. There was dried blood on his chin. "I smell it, too. What the hell is it?"

Kit gave Jordy a nudge.

"I'm getting up. Damn."

Kit started rolling her side of the sleeping bag, then she grabbed the end of the double foam and lifted. A sharp, ammonia-like odour knocked her backwards. "It's the foams! We sweat right through them and they're stinking up the room!"

Clark kicked out of the sleeping bag, rolled off the foam and bent, his nose almost touching the floor's white surface. "The smell's gone right into the floor!"

"Jesus on a roller skate!" Kit cried. "Now what?"

"Open the windows," Clark ordered, waving his hands to create a weak breeze. "Let's get some air moving in here."

Jordy and Kit cranked open windows, while Clark stuffed his legs into yesterday's pants. "Maybe there's something to clean with." He motioned to the cupboards beneath the wet bar.

Chantal was swinging doors open. Glasses, liquor, crackers. She tried the last cupboard. "Windex!"

"And paper towel," Jordy added, grabbing the roll.

Kit was afraid to try it. "It might discolour the floor."

"Try a test spot, over there, in the corner behind the water cooler," Clark said.

Kit scrabbled across the floor on her knees and gave a quick spray. "It's okay."

"Does it take the smell out?" Chantal asked.

She bent and sniffed. "It minimizes it. Quick ... get that all in the van while I clean. Do you think they're up yet? God, they can't come in here now—"

"Holy rankness." Jordy grabbed the end of his sleeping bag and started rolling. "They'll think we peed ourselves."

Kit sprayed and scrubbed, stuffing the used paper towel into her knapsack while her family scurried around her. "Shit! There's not even a whiff of a breeze."

The foams and sleeping bags were cleared out. Jordy and Clark moved the heavy glass table and patio chairs back into place. Laurent was coming up the pool-house steps, dressed for work in neat tan slacks and a short-sleeved shirt with the sleeves rolled a half turn. "You'll stay for breakfast, yes?" he was saying. "Isabel has fruit and bagels, and the coffee's on."

Clark jumped on this. "Thanks, but no. You've been so kind, opening your home to us like this, but we've got a lot of miles to put on again today."

"Okay, brother." Laurent took Clark's hand in both of his. He called into the house, in French, and Isabel appeared at the door.

"You're leaving already?"

"Have to. Newfoundland or bust," Kit said. "Thank you so much for the hospitality."

Isabel kissed her on both cheeks and hugged her hard. She did the same to Clark and the children.

Laurent glanced at his watch. "I have to go now. You want to follow me back to the highway?"

"Good idea," Clark said.

They piled into the van. Clark had the windows down and the radio cranked before Laurent could detect the ticking.

"Goodbye! Good luck!" Isabel was waving from the front door. "*Au revoir!*"

They backed out. "Thank Christ," Clark said. He was sure he'd aged ten years overnight. His chipped teeth were paining him, the nerves exposed. Hot and cold were going to be a bitch.

∼

In Ontario there are Parliament Hill adventures. Logan has a snake encounter in Algonquin Park — contrary to popular belief, garter snakes *do* bite. The kids fish whenever possible, and we hike along the shores of frigid Great Lakes.

Quebec City serves up a summer festival, seventeenth-century architecture and cobblestoned walks. We regret that we've never learned more than high school French.

In New Brunswick we sleep in a gas station parking lot because all the campgrounds are full. We gaze in awe at the Hopewell Rocks, suffer a van breakdown in the Bay of Fundy, and get thoroughly lost in Moncton — twice.

We mail postcards from the lighthouse at Peggy's Cove, Nova Scotia, buy saltwater taffy in Lunenburg, and happen onto the set of the now-cancelled CBC TV series *Black Harbour* in Hubbards. We just miss seeing Sylvester Stallone — also on vacation — in Halifax, but I may have seen Rita MacNeil in a Toyota.

Cape Breton offers amazing views, cliff-diving, ceilidhs, and a whaling tour: I won tickets for the tour in a campground raffle.

∼

They adored Old Quebec. The little shops and outdoor cafés, the cobblestone streets, the busy St. Lawrence, where tugboats, sailboats, cruise ships and Sea-Doos shared the water below the green hills of the historic Plains of Abraham. They'd inadvertently arrived on the last day of the International Summer Festival—buskers, jugglers, musicians, and happy crowds everywhere. They watched a mime in a top hat with silver-painted skin move in extra slow motion. A Peruvian band played on the boardwalk near the Chateau Frontenac: they bought the CD.

Jordy had a mad on because Clark wouldn't let him spend $30 on a switchblade, but the children were otherwise content, and full with the day.

Next stop: New Brunswick, with luck, before dark.

Kit shuffled the maps on her lap, flipped through the CAA campground book. They drove in silence. She stared out the window as they passed neat little villages and dairy farms.

"What are you thinking about?" Clark asked. He used his knuckles to scratch beneath his nose.

What was there to say? She could hear her husband breathing, her daughter turning another page in her book. Kit considered her situation: she was thirty-six years old, a mother of two, a dabbler in paint and people, travelling east on the TransCanada beneath a low-slung sky. "We forgot to drink the beer."

"The Big Rock?" Clark probed the chipped teeth with his tongue, wincing as wires of pain shot through.

"Yep. It's still in the pool house, beside the door." She sighed. "I'm going to take some photos of the Quebec countryside. Maybe I'll paint this when we get back. Chantal, is my camera back there?"

Chantal dug among the bags and passed her mother the Canon. The girl had drawn her own map, in blue ballpoint, up her arm to her elbow.

Kit rolled the window two thirds down. The sky was the colour of milk. She wasn't sure anything would turn out, but she balanced the camera on the glass, focused on a dairy barn, and snapped.

~

We cross the Confederation Bridge into PEI, buy potatoes at the first roadside stand, and spend night one at Seal Cove, a site that lives up to its name. In Cavendish we queue for a campsite and pay for a record *four* glorious nights in one spot. We cycle along the red cliffs, tour the Anne of Green Gables estate, stroll through Charlottetown and quaint seaside towns.

The night ferry to Newfoundland is a gas: everyone literally racing for the best place to bed down with pillows and blankets. An old couple beside me converse in Gaelic. A few days later our children practically stumble into a moose in Terra Nova National Park — no harm done. We eat fish and chips with the locals, pose for photos beside a Beech 18 at the North Atlantic Aviation Museum in Gander, ramble around St. John's famous George Street in the rain. And yes, we reach the end of the continent: Cape Spear. 'Tis a strange thing to be closer to Ireland than home.

New friends … capital cities … road squabbles (Do YOU want to drive?) … the raging Atlantic … van breakdowns … we add these adventures to our life list. In British Columbia, a few years before, we'd beachcombed near Tofino, swum across the swim-for-your-life Similkameen River, and endured a bizarre and unplanned cycling excursion through the hectic centre of Vancouver.

Alberta's given us Banff, Calgary, Jasper, Edmonton, and Kananaskis Country, where a park warden informed us that we'd narrowly missed meeting a grizzly upon our cycling path.

We've done it now. We've completed our self-imposed parental responsibility. With my husband driving and me as chief navigator, our children have had a good glimpse at this country, but after five weeks of gadding about in the east, we've missed the prairie's line-straight horizon and the names of towns that slide off our tongues. We find ourselves searching vehicles for green and white licence plates.

In Spanish, Ontario, what stood out was not the fact that we stumbled onto an unbelievably fine campground with two waterfalls, but that we met a couple there from Neilburg, Saskatchewan, who had known my husband's grandfather when he was the butcher in that town. And as much as I loved riding the cold Atlantic waves in Cape Breton, what really delighted was the young man who spotted my grey University of Saskatchewan Huskies' sweatshirt and asked if I'd attended the U of S, as he had. In PEI, a cute teen on the beach approached my son with, "You look familiar ..." and they discovered they'd both attended Camp Kinasao at Christopher Lake, Saskatchewan.

It was a race to get back home, and when we reached the Saskatchewan border we stopped for one more MasterCard moment: the children clung to that welcome sign like a lifeboat. True, we can't claim an ocean, and our nearest mountain is man-made, but what we've learned is that Saskatchewan is one-of-a-kind, and we wouldn't trade her in, B'y, we wouldn't let her go.

~

They'd do Fredericton tomorrow and camp in or near Moncton. There was a huge water park there with screamer slides, and Magnetic Hill. The tidal bore. The kids would like it.

Clark was playing with the radio dial, finding only French. He plugged in one of the compilation tapes he'd made for the journey. This was the music they'd fallen in love to—tThe Police, Foreigner, The Eagles—songs that had taken them through the baby years, their first apartment, all the major tragedies and minor successes that'd added up and help to shape the neurotic pair they'd become.

Clark looked at Kit. Her hair was blowing, and she was trying to batten it down with one hand so it wouldn't fly before the viewfinder and ruin her shot. He could already see her running into the frigid Atlantic with the kids, and squealing as the waves knocked her down; being the first one up to dance at a Cape Breton ceilidh; finding the best stones on the rocky beaches of Newfoundland and naming them—Moon Shower, Old Man Laughing—as she turned them like charms in her hands.

His father was a damn fool.

Kit handed the camera back to Chantal. Clark was driving like a woman again. She bit off a smile. Then she plucked his right hand off the wheel, kissed his wrist, and watched him mouth the words of a song he would not now or ever sing.

I WASN'T ALWAYS LIKE THIS

I AM A THIRTY-NINE-YEAR-OLD WOMAN, IN LOVE WITH my husband and having fun with my teenagers, and I have just bought myself a house away from them all. But today, the day after I signed the deposit cheque and lined up a lawyer, I am headed in a different direction: I am four hours west and north of the city that's been making me crazy, raw nerve by raw nerve.

My daughter Taylor has turned sixteen, and to celebrate she's invited five friends to the northern Saskatchewan lake where my parents own a cottage. We call it the *family cabin*. *Family*, because we all — my parents, four siblings, a rodeo of dogs, and my own family — take advantage of it, but really, it belongs to my folks. *Cabin*, because in Saskatchewan that's what we call a cottage. On a Friday at 5:00 p.m., Taylor and company squeeze into our minivan and we make for Greig Lake in the Meadow Lake Provincial Park. The girls sing, pop heads out the window, maniacally wave at people in other vehicles.

Some of these friends have never been to this part of Saskatchewan. When we leave the mostly tree-barren prairie and enter the moody Northern Provincial Forest, I ask them to watch for deer; we just miss hitting five.

At dusk we arrive at the squat log cabin two rows back from the lake to learn there's a boil water advisory in effect. Cryptosporidium and its cousins make everyone fearful. The water is not hooked up; a kind neighbour shares from his cache. We fill jugs for drinking water, carry dish and wash-water from the lake. No one minds the hauling.

After spending a late night with a rented video — typical Hollywood teen fare these girls, all in an accelerated-school-program, brought with them — I've awoken knowing with utter certainty that buying the house was the right thing to do. I did not know until now.

It's been variously said — and famously so by Virginia Woolf — that every woman writer needs a room of her own.

I had a room.

It was not enough.

~

The girls shimmy into bathing suits, grab books and a beach ball, and spend hours beside the lake that's still mostly wearing its lid of ice. They are reading *The Vagina Monologues*, and *The Celestine Prophecy*, and old *Archie* comics. Someone's unearthed a water-damaged Harlequin Romance. They read the juicy parts aloud.

I join them on the beach with my camera and black-and-white film, say I'd like to interview each of them about their lives now and where they expect to be in ten years.

We'll have a reunion when they're twenty-six. (These are the kinds of things I think about.) The girls approve of the idea but no one wants to do it right this minute, and before the weekend folds itself up, the opportunity will pass.

~

In our inner-city neighbourhood there's at least one artist, student, professional, senior, and addict on every block. As a writer of literary books — and other things that actually pay, including articles for the *Western Producer* and short humorous pieces for CBC Radio Saskatchewan — I fit in. But the city also turns me inside out: the noise, the crime, the busyness. When Frank and Margaret — the elderly Mennonite couple who lived next to us for a decade — moved on, the house was purchased as a revenue property and the troubles began.

Always, it's been young men. Drinking. Drugs. Dangerous driving. Coming and going through the devil's hours of the night. I haven't slept properly in my own home for years. Aside from the pair who *really* trashed the basement suite — and blared gangster rap day and night, left hypodermics in my flowerbed, and skipped from province to province fleeing arrest warrants — I likely don't have any reason to fear the convoy of punks who park in our spot, deliberately cross our front lawn, shatter beer bottles, and whoop, yell, and knock on our windows via the shared sidewalk between our houses (where they occasionally relieve themselves). They haven't threatened me or anyone in my family, but I sense the potential for violence (there *was* the beer-swigging trio who chucked machetes around the yard after they hacked down Frank and Margaret's beloved crabapple tree).

I fear for my teenagers, who often traverse the corridor at night, my husband, who recently confronted a half dozen of the neighbouring miscreants, and I fear for my own body, mind, and spirit.

Something terrible is imminent.

~

A car screams down my street. I hear doors slam. *Wazzz up?* Fuck this and that and you. Stupid-drunk girls. Rowdy boyfriends. Fighting.

I bolt to the window and one-eye-peek through thick curtains. I keep doors locked, check and double-check before I use my front door or step out back to the English country garden — replete with cattails surrounding the pond, Chinese lanterns that really do seem to contain a glowing light, woodland anemones, unfurling ferns, and open-armed hosta. Here Russian Giant sunflowers have reached fourteen feet, and a Virginia creeper obscures the neighbouring yard and keeps up the pretense of an urban oasis in the core of Bridge City. I've been a gardener since I was a child, and this fragrant, painterly garden has so often sustained me. We built a six-foot privacy fence, but relaxing beneath the shade of the lilac — my favourite spot in the world; chickadees visit at 4:00 p.m. — remains out of the question. If I know the neighbours are outside, or might *come* outside, or have just *been* outside, I barricade myself *inside*. I'm a self-styled hostage.

This paralyzing fear once led me to move in with my mother-in-law for five days. I was a weeping basket case.

Couldn't work. Couldn't concentrate. Couldn't be a regular human being. What was wrong with me?

My Internet diagnosis — we're *all* doctors now — confirms that I share characteristics synonymous with paranoid personality disorder; chiefly, my constant suspicion that my neighbours have sinister motives. But there are big buts: I don't have excessive trust in my own knowledge and abilities, don't avoid close relationships with others, don't search for hidden meanings in everything, don't challenge the loyalties of friends and loved ones, and don't, I hope, appear cold and distant to others.

Perhaps I'm not paranoid after all. But what am I? Clearly, I am something.

One troubled season has held hands with the next.

~

Spring 2002. I was perilously close to the edge, and although I'd hoped to sail through this life without drugs or psychiatric help, I succumbed to the former. How many times could I break down in my basement and scream at my husband: *T, you don't understand?* I resented him for *Not Doing Something.*

Is menopause to blame? At thirty-six I'd had a cancer scare and underwent an emergency surgery to remove two softball-sized tumours in my abdomen. The tumours were sent to a lab in Vancouver for testing, and we waited. It was December; I wept at my daughter's Christmas concert. The results came back two weeks later: benign, thank you, Jesus. The surgeon had also performed a bilateral salpingo-oophorectomy: an across-the-board evisceration of all things reproductive. The latter was done for safety's sake, and it catapulted me into radical menopause, complete with the much-maligned hot flashes and worsened insomnia. Menopause is a kind of scapegoat; one can attribute all kinds of miseries to it.

Or maybe I'm just going nuts: mental illness is the skeleton in our familial closet. Numerous suicides, including my grandfather's barn-hanging on a Hallowe'en night — one of three siblings who took their own lives—when my father was a boy, and a first cousin's carbon monoxide poisoning.

Breathe, I tell myself when I feel that familiar dread mounting. *In, out. In, out.* I repeat simple mantras. *Blue skies. Blue skies. Blue skies.* Good efforts, but damn it: not nearly enough.

And now I take drugs. "Mother's Little Helpers," as Mick Jagger and the boys put it. The pills aid my journey to the good country: sleep.

~

I needed to break out of the prison of my thoughts. But go where? My husband and I had scoured the newspaper's real estate section, dreaming of acreages. Who were we kidding? I'm a writer of non-bestselling, small press books, and T earns a small income cleaning surgical equipment: acreages don't exist in our universe.

I thought that maybe we should just sell our house and buy another. Nope, couldn't do that. Despite what happened around its perimeter, I was connected to the old mongrel of a home, with its slanting floors and leaky roof, its windows that welcomed winter winds to breeze right through them, and sometimes had me sleeping in a toque. I'd suffered numerous nightmares about selling the City Park house. I'd be traumatized to pass by one day and see another family watching a thunderstorm play out from the verandah, or see my tiger lilies uprooted beside the front step. The home, the only one my children had ever known, had been a harbour in a storm-tossed sea of a life — years saturated with mental and occasionally marital turmoil — and there was not a surface we hadn't sanded, painted or patched with our own hands, using money we'd scraped together in blistered fits and starts. We'd placed so many personal time capsules in the walls, we couldn't begin to remember where we'd hidden them all.

I felt doomed. Then one morning I split the newspaper, spread it like a map across the dining room table, and spied an ad for *Saskatchewan's Best Kept Secret*: a cheap house on a private lot in a small town, an hour and a half from Saskatoon. A mere ten-minute walk from a lake. I called, we looked, I made an offer. Done.

~

I wasn't always like this. One thing that put me at ease was leaving the city; fortunately, work takes me away often. Giving readings and workshops, mostly. I earn much of my living presenting my poetry and prose in schools and libraries. A few months ago, after delivering a day-long writing workshop in a small town — and getting zero sleep the night before thanks to the all-night bash next door — I detoured to visit a friend in the country. She has her own problems: single parent, struggling writer, a court case over the farm property she's splitting with her ex. Still she bakes bread. Still she listens to my rants.

She met me outside, brunette hair Godiva-like as she led me up the stairs and past the latest episode of kittens. "I'm behind," she said, clearing dirty plates from the table. "Please forgive the mess."

It felt like home should be.

Artist Mary J. Blige sings: "Leave your situations at the door." I wanted to. I wish I could have dropped my emotional baggage at the door: or even further, back in the city, but this was not possible.

"So how've you been?" My friend opened one of the warm beer I'd brought. Labatt Light.

Truthfully, I hate to complain and I dislike complainers. Without any real attempt, I've managed to socially surround myself with positive, upbeat people. Shiny, happy people; another song.

I told her everything. I purged about my life as a prisoner in my own house, my emotional darkness, and my desire to run away to a small country where I didn't speak the language and could exist on bread and cheese. One floor below us, her teenaged son and his band played "Californication" on drums and electric guitars. Before long, the boys surfaced from the basement. An emaciated adolescent with long hair the colour of corn had dough and instructions for baking-powder biscuits.

It was dizzying. The cacophony of plates and cutlery. Thunderous music. My friend making a whopping amount of spaghetti and meat sauce for this ravenous party of rock-and-rollers. Then the phone rang. "It's for you," my friend said. My husband had news: the neighbouring landlord had evicted the hellions. Great news, but both T and I knew that the obnoxious neighbours were only part of the problem; I'd still have to get away.

After dishes, my friend and I went back-roading. Like teenagers ourselves, we each stuffed a bottle of beer into our jacket pockets and climbed into her half-ton to tour the hills where she lives and rents out farmland.

I have yet to mention the drought, Saskatchewan's worst since the 1930s. We rode around inspecting the damage, the cartoonish tumbleweeds, topsoil peeling away from the land like burnt skin. Eventually we arrived at an abandoned farmhouse and sat in the surrounding brome. My friend rolled a joint. I sipped my beer, and we perused the prairie night sky. She pointed out Venus, Saturn, and Mercury. I didn't care if she wasn't right.

We sat in the grey-boned company of that homestead for hours: two middle-aged women beneath our other friend, the moon.

And coyotes sang.

And we talked about why we are the way we are. Scoured our childhoods for early signs.

~

I spent part of my childhood in comically named Turtleford: three years that were anything but funny to me.

It goes back a terminally long way. Back to being five, six, seven. Back to daily being chased by a posse of older boys; they hid among balers and combines in the farm equipment lot I had to cross to get to school.

Back to getting caught.

Often.

~

The girls are delightful.

Bright, untroubled, beautiful, with their long legs and flawless skin. At any given moment they might break into song, or tackle one another, or ask if they can help with anything. They are the kind of kids who ask how your day is going and really, really care. This daughter of mine — against all odds and smothering overprotection — is right as rain.

The girls prepare for a forest hike. I offer an empty plastic pop bottle and ask them to add a few rocks to make a shaker. "Something to alert the bears with." While they're gone, I take two lawn chairs (one for a leg prop) and a manuscript I'm editing onto the deck.

Oh, sun, you've been missed. It's intoxicating to be out with the blue jays and pileated woodpeckers, and light so dazzling it's almost its own emotion.

Oh, May. All praise and glory to you.

~

My husband: *You're splitting us up.*

Me: *Wrong… I'm keeping us together. Me together.*

We both knew I had to have it. I'd spent my adult life scrimping — second-hand clothes, used furniture, cutting my own hair — but had gradually managed to save just what was needed: $20,000.

Of course I couldn't have picked a worse time, but is there ever a good or right time for anything? Having babies?

Taking holidays? Dying? We spend too much time planning, not enough following those instinctive animals we know as our guts.

I bought the house for a song. And it awaits.

∼

The girls are still hiking. Alone at the cabin for these few hours, with this gift of full sun, I could weep for all that's ahead of me. Solitude, and my own furniture. My own yard. The requisite planting around the house; the flower beds appear to have been neglected for years. A wood stove. Rooms that require throw rugs. And paint.

Right now it's just the dog — Alex Trebek — and me: he's on pills, too. Hip dysplasia. My running partner for eight years, he's old now, and sad about his decline. I think he also feels somewhat guilty.

Alex, I bought my own house, I tell him. *A house by a lake.*

Alex is my best friend; he totally gets it.

∼

We construct a campfire, though we keep it small — with the drought and all things poised to explode into flame, I don't want to be responsible for reducing the forest to ashes.

The girls have brought Jersey Milk bars, marshmallows, and graham wafers. We make s'mores. Chocolate is a good thing.

And there is effervescent laughter.

And bat sightings.

Michael Jackson-esque dancing.

And campfire smoke in our hair.

Perhaps — as my son once suggested while lying in a field beneath the Perseids — this is as good as it gets.

~

June now, and I'm improving. No anxiety attacks for weeks, no need for the grace of small blue pills.

My books are still not making waves, the sky's not yet releasing rain, but the wind lifts the white lace I've draped across the window in my modest home away. A trio of rabbits is running figure-eights on the lawn, and I have the glorious woods as neighbours. I've become a woman who sits beside a window and finds bliss in looking out.

Virginia, I think it's enough.

CALLE 55

NOTES FROM AN EXCHANGE

Greetings from Hotel San Juan.

It's 5:40 a.m., my windows are open to the morning, and it smells like rain. In my three and a half weeks in Mexico it has rained only once, but it was a downpour, a baptism, and one of the Canadians — Rosalie, a photographer — danced in the puddles like a child, happy in her feet.

We dance often here — in the streets, where a different band plays salsa or merengue on each block and people of all ages not only move but manage to *become* the music; in clubs, where we might hear the same songs five or six times a night and no one would dream of complaining; in our rooms, if Laura (pronounced La-ora), easily the best dancer among the Mexicans, offers an impromptu salsa lesson. Shoes are kicked off, beds pushed aside. Another *buen día* in Mérida.

When I see myself in photographs or catch a glimpse in the mirror, I wonder: *Who is this woman, smiling all the time?*

I left my husband and teenaged children in autumn-dreary Saskatoon, where the cool weather mirrored my disposition. I left a manic schedule that included numerous school tours, leading creative writing workshops, editing, freelancing, and the simultaneous writing of my next two books. I left the absolute drudgery of washing floors, doing endless loads of laundry, cleaning the dog's kennel. I left exhaustion and bitterness. Just surviving each day was so much work. And even though I rarely took time off, I only ever had just enough money to pay my bills. Clearly, I was adrift — this Mexican adventure was a life raft.

In order to make the separation complete, I told my family I would not be contacting them in the month I would be away, except through very occasional e-mails.

This two-part exchange, sponsored by the Banff Centre of the Arts and FONCA (*Fondo Nacional para la Cultura y las Artes*), integrates countries, disciplines, and cultures. Next year: six weeks in Banff. Before I left, a producer at CBC Radio Saskatchewan called to ask if I would phone in weekly reports from Mérida: absolutely not. If I was not going to be conversing with my family, I was certainly not going to speak to anyone else.

The Canadians (five photographers, five writers) arrived October 15, 2002 to a city in ruins. Mérida — Yucatán capital and a high-spirited city of one million — is recovering from the aftermath of Hurricane Isadore, which devastated roads, buildings, trees and lives. An estimated 500,000 Yucatecos are homeless. Three died.

The graceful city I had explored many times via the Internet was not the city I arrived in, yet as I piled into a taxi with three other Canadians, I had the distinct sense that for the first time in my thirty-nine years, I was home.

This is my second visit to Mexico. I have also spent brief amounts of time in the Dominican Republic (1987) and Venezuela (1997). The euphoria I'm feeling in Mérida is similar to the emotions I experienced in those other countries: beyond joy. I am floating.

The Canadian participants rendezvoused in the hotel lobby that first evening. The ten Mexican writers and photographers — from Mexico City, Mérida, Mazatlán and Comalcalco, Tabasco — were not around. This may have been a good thing. I was disoriented enough as I settled into my hotel room — two single beds with bright orange quilts, a fan, a dresser with an elaborately carved mirror frame — and met the other Canadian artists.

Our initial meeting with the Mexican contingent occurred, perhaps symbolically, on a dark street. We introduced ourselves and shook hands, as if in a receiving line — *mucho gusto, encantada* — then dined in an outdoor café with music, roaming street vendors, begging grandmothers, and fits and starts of Spanglish weaving multi-coloured threads through our first of many surreal nights.

From my landing in Cancún and bus ride to Mérida until this very moment, as I'm scribbling these notes, I have remained in a state of acute sensitivity. Colours and images are vibrant; every sound — even the constant jackhammering in the streets — reaches my ears as music.

I sat between Laura and Gerardo — two of the *intercambio*'s young Mexican photographers recognized as among the finest of their generation. I don't remember the conversation, but we raised our glasses together — *salud* — and smiled *frecuentemente*. I knew this was going to be great.

Half the Mexican participants speak good or excellent English, the others speak little or none. I had decided before I came that I would I use as much Spanish as possible. I believed I was prepared; I've studied Spanish off and on since 1987 and arrived with at least enough skill for *conversaciones breves*. I know how to conjugate. I possess a decent vocabulary. Yet I tremble and inadvertently close my ears when anyone speaks Spanish to me. *Un problema muy grande.* A full-fledged phobia. I manage well in restaurants and stores, but discussions among this group of brilliant, educated and predominantly young intellectuals quickly rises to levels I have no words for — sometimes, I fear, in *any* language.

Why does this happen to me? I want more than anything to be able to comprehend Spanish. Maybe I want it too much. I'm so afraid of failure I can't even hear. I cannot imagine having arrived here with no knowledge of the language, as some of my associates have. At least I can *speak* Spanish, even if I understand only a morsel of what's being said.

～

Mérida, rebuilding.

There is much to do. Trees as wide as Volkswagens have been plucked from the ground. Branches litter the sprawling city. I have seen aluminum roofing dangling in treetops. Concrete's tumbled, windows are smashed, but nothing I see compares to the ruined streets. It would be easy to die here: to avoid toppling into a crater is only half of it. Crossing a street without being smeared — by bus, car or tearing *ambulancia* — or being crushed by the crowds on the narrow sidewalks, or dissolving in the oppressive heat of the *mercado*, where you jostle shoulder to elbow to knee with other shoppers, are blurrier matters.

Yet I feel safe here. Safer walking alone on the streets at 2:00 a.m. than I would feel in my own city — in my own neighbourhood! — at dusk. A strong police presence helps, but there is also a general feeling that no harm can come to me here.

Mérida is cosmopolitan and ancient, garishly rich and desperately poor. Founded in 1542 by the Spaniard Francisco de Montejo (a popular beer is among his legacies), it was once a large Mayan city known as T'ho. After the Spanish conquest — the particularly long and bloody battle is depicted in numerous murals inside the Palacio de Gobierno — the Mayan temples and palaces were dismantled and the stones were used as the foundation for the Cathedral of San Idelfonso, located in Mérida's main plaza. Spanish and French colonial architecture, as well as Moorish influences, are evident throughout the city, especially along Paseo Montejo, the elegant, tree-lined street that runs like a long vein toward the city's historic heart.

Mérida is clowns with enormous balloon bouquets. It's horse-drawn carriages, soldiers on parade, lovers on park benches, blaring sirens, little girls dolled up like princesses, road repair crews, schoolgirls in tartan skirts, blouses white and crisp as sails, Spanish-speaking Mennonites selling cheese, shoe shiners, street musicians, salsa dancers, sprawling markets. I see newspapers and sweets sold on street corners, vendors pitching *hamacas*, fans, Panama hats, beggars with physical deformities, bats as big as pigeons, Mayan women in traditional white dresses with elaborately embroidered flowers at the neck and hem, live outdoor theatre, magic. How can any season in Saskatoon compare?

The Yucatán is rich in Mayan tradition. It's dotted with *ruinas*, some 3000 *cenotes* (sink holes), *pueblos*, low and high jungle, almost deserted coastal villages, un-Americanized beaches, thin dogs, plazas with centuries-old *catedrales* on one side, government buildings on the other. *Tiendas*, *restaurantes*, *parques*, *panaderías*, *lavanderías*, *peluquerías*, *mercados*, *escuelas*, *papelerías*, *universidades*, *cantinas*, *museos*, *haciendas*, *galerías*, and *casas* at both ends of the economic scale fill in the gaps. Stores that sell material and Christmas wrapping paper are big here. As are saints.

Although I am not Catholic, I am spiritually moved by the outward signs of faith the mostly Catholic Mexicans exhibit. People of all ages genuflect and kiss their hand when they pass cathedrals. I spend a fair amount of time in cathedrals, too, feeling like a little girl. I am in awe of the elaborate architecture; votive candles; old men on their knees, praying. I try to pray, but am so overwhelmed I'm unable to concentrate. Perhaps this is prayer enough.

In several of the small towns we've visited, I've seen folks riding three-wheeled, canopied bikes with a seat in front for passengers or packages. I have seen ladders transported this way, even a boat floating sideways down a street.

My experience in the Yucatán has been perpetually hallucinatory. I am in a constant state of *pinch me*. I keep expecting to wake up, hoping I never do.

Saskatchewan and the Yucatán: it's impossible to fathom that the two exist in the same world. Everything I have experienced here — from the food to the weather — is so radically different, it might be another planet.

~

The structure of this exchange is that there is no structure. For some this has been incredibly frustrating; for others, like me, it's been one of the highlights. What is meant to happen is collaboration and the creation of art. But how to begin?

During the first few days, in the lavish Teatro Mérida, the photographers gave slide presentations and the writers spoke about their work. I recited a poem, "*Vestidos Sencillos*" ("Simple Dresses"), that had come to me, in Spanish, back in Saskatchewan. I explained, in Spanish and English, that being in Mexico to write and collaborate with Mexican artists was the dream I'd been having my entire life. On the stage I felt a surge of emotion and could not avoid tears. Maleea, a young poet from Victoria, also cried during her talk. We have become close friends.

The presentations required lengthy translations, and afterwards we left en masse to eat. Twenty-two people dining together in Mexico can seem like a lifetime. The

Mexicans were helpful, suggesting what we might order, naming the free appetizers as they arrived, plate after plate, demonstrating the proper way to fold tortillas. Will we be as generous when they come to Canada next year? They've made maps to help us locate economical restaurants. They offer Spanish lessons, and assist us at the bank.

But we are a crowd of twenty-two. Every little thing takes so much time and I am accustomed to bolting. By the third day I only wanted to be alone. Too much talking, too much waiting, too much standing around. And the heat! I swim through the air, and my clothes fuse to my skin.

Enough of *el grupo*: I found refuge in a park — think pavement, not grass, a few huge trees with their bases painted white — near our hotel. Except when touring, I am a woman who spends much time alone. I require absolute silence to think and write and adequately recognize what I'm feeling. My teens and husband are usually gone all day; the quiet and solitude are blissful.

The sun began to set. Couples began congregating in the park, and — apparently oblivious to anyone else — made as much love as is physically possible when fully clothed on a public park bench. They sank into each other's arms and eyes. Fingers trailed through dark hair. They kissed as though living the lyrics of one of the songs I've learned to dance to: *I want to eat your mouth and never breathe again.*

From those early evenings sprang the idea for my first collaboration. I asked Gerardo to help me interview and photograph couples on park benches; back in Saskatoon I will fabricate stories for each of them. We had to wait several minutes for our first passionate couple to come up for air.

"*How long have you been together?*" I asked. "*Dos horas.*" Two hours? They'd just met via the Internet.

There were many more meetings in dark, airless restaurants with *el grupo*; we have thankfully finished these now. I often found the presentations academic, and then there were questions, and the necessary translating. I was anxious and frustrated. The small rooms felt claustrophobic. When it was my night I clipped it short. The heat. We chalk many things up to the heat.

At night, with the fan whirring above me, I sleep without dreams.

Duermo como una angelita.

~

Music is the current that runs through everything here, and in the beginning I was going slightly *loca* with my desire to dance and no one to dance with. On the fourth night, a small group of us went out to a Cuban club, and as we danced we could almost hear the ice shattering around our feet. After that night: much more dancing. As long as I live, I will never forget Azul Picante, an unadorned, second-floor club with a live band and a small, wizened woman selling paper towels in the washroom.

Many tight friendships have followed.

I've connected with Maleea and Mexicans Juan José and Andrés (fiction writers), plus Gerardo (photographer). We are *la familia*. As the days melt together we explore the Yucatán in rented Nissans and cluster in sidewalk cafés. We talk about living as artists in Canada and Mexico. What's different, what's the same. (In Mexico the artists rely even more heavily on the generous prizes and grants available; their government appears much more artist-friendly than my own.) We speak mostly Spanish. We eat. Once, after I'd eaten all I believed possible of my fish in a fly-infested market in Progreso, the nearest coastal town, Andrés asked if I was done and proceeded to devour the head. We take our photos together. We translate each other's work. We travel beach to beach, and laugh all the time.

The Canadians take turns being sick. Maleea says we spend the first two weeks arriving, the last two trying not to leave.

~

The photographers work harder than the writers. We scribble impressions — mine in three notebooks, on a laptop computer I balance on my knees (there are no desks provided), on scraps of paper, napkins, the palm of my left hand — and soak up experiences for future reference. The photographers need to get it on film *now*.

By the end of the second week, several collaborations are in progress.

It's all an exchange; there is no way to do this wrong. I don't yet know what shape my exchange-inspired work will take. I live each day in Mexico to the fullest. I learn, and sweat, and dance, and trip. I record more impressions, and take photographs, and try to freeze time.

I don't attend everything — there are dinners, exhibitions and day trips — and I don't form a personal relationship with each of the participants. There are a few I have scarcely spoken to, others who will be lifelong friends.

One of the women has become depressed, a condition I can empathize with, yet I selfishly make no effort to become her friend. I am at the other extreme here. I don't want anything to interfere with the perfection my life has become.

~

There is much more to tell — the jungle, the ruins, the Day of the Dead, flamingos, a badly taped Doors cassette, walking in shadows, swimming in a punchbowl for snakes, the hours of just being together and not saying anything at all — but now it is almost 10:30 a.m., and time to eat.

I will say hello to Faosto and Ebam at the front desk as I leave my key. I will step onto Calle 55 and swim again through the thick morning heat toward a breakfast of yogurt *con fruta y granola*. I will hold a cup of *té negro* in my hands and try not to think about the few days left. I will attempt, again, to convince myself: *This is real. This is real. This is real.*

It is hard not to feel profound sadness, as well, for I have learned a painful truth: I do not miss home. Here, I am happy right through to my bones, with these people whom I hardly know at all. I want the members of my family back home to experience this elation in their own lives, however or wherever it might occur for them. It doesn't seem fair that it is mine alone.

As some people feel they were born in the wrong body, I feel that this place is where I was meant to be. I could lose the map here. But not yet. I am still a mother. I have responsibilities. I have commitments. I have a great big life in Canada to walk back into, and the people there who love me haven't heard my voice in weeks.

A TALE OF TWO GARDENS

IT WAS THE BEST OF TIMES, IT WAS THE WORST OF TIMES...
Several years ago, my husband and I hosted a demolition party. Every able-bodied person on our Saskatoon block — both the young, and those who could remember when Barbie couldn't bend her legs — was welcomed to take a sledgehammer whack to our dilapidated garage. There was beer, a soundtrack. It made for an excellent home video. At the end of the day we were left with an island of concrete — a hefty foot thick — and an expensive, one-day jackhammer rental.

These were the kinds of things we did to ourselves.

After the ton of rubble was cleared (now *there* was a weight-loss program) and a load of fresh topsoil delivered, we set out to transform our neglected inner-city yard into a garden oasis — a refuge, if you will: feast for the eyes, balm for the soul, resort for feathered friends. We shaped and sculpted, planted and pruned. Mother Nature helped with a few exceedingly wet springs, and our labours were well-rewarded.

From the vantage of my second-floor office window, the winding flagstone path resembled a slightly alien woman, running. A natural pond sheathed in lily pads and surrounded by cattails, arrowhead, and spotted water-hemlock culled from prairie sloughs was home to thirty happy goldfish — including Bertha, the matriarch — and a few suckers from the South Saskatchewan River. The trickling waterfall attracted the usual volery of robins, finches, and chickadees, but it also seduced northern juncos, rose-breasted and evening grosbeaks, and a shockingly bright (and perhaps lost) western tanager. In the beginning, I didn't know a sparrow from a wren.

It was the spring of hope…

We cut an amazing deal on odds-and-ends patio bricks in a variety of hues, which, when wedged into place, looked like Pez candies a child had lined up for fun.

Soon the garden was a conflagration of perennials: lupins, peonies, poppies, lilies, forget-me-nots, daisies and ethereal flax. My husband's grandmother's ferns. (Say *that* three times fast!) There were pink hollyhocks from a farmer friend. Several varieties of lamium from the crop scientist down the street. We'd been encouraging Virginia creeper to wind its tendrilous way over our six-foot privacy fence, so that one day we'd be well and truly cloaked in verdancy.

Ah, nature's *otherworld*. The very antithesis of the hustle and tussle of our workaday lives. It was spirit-lifting to lounge in the Muskoka chairs beneath the lilac's long arms of shade, and dismiss the truth that we were only a few blocks from downtown Saskatoon (though frequent sirens from nearby City Hospital tended to jolt us from utopian reveries).

The only lawn in our urban yard was a postage stamp in front, and we considered even that too much. We'd quickly grown to disdain lawn — in *anyone's* yard — and couldn't imagine why all and sundry didn't plow theirs up in favour of a bush, shade plant, and floral *mélange*. If a Russian giant sunflower decided to rise up from among our brown-eyed Susans, so be it. The woodland anenome felt like creeping toward the Chinese lanterns, no problem. In short, we'd become garden snobs, and *lawn, grass,* and *turf* no longer existed in our lexicon.

But something strange occurred.

I purchased a modest house — a go-anytime writing retreat — in a village northeast and not far from Saskatoon.

It was the winter of despair...

The 60-by-140-foot lot was bordered by privacy-providing lilacs, elms, spruce, aspen, poplar, caraganas, mountain ash, and a Russian olive I was particularly fond of. Here squirrels played tag and birds sang arias in the woods — real, storybook woods — that backstopped the yard. If one meandered along the narrow path between the woodland and a barley field, cut through the luminous clearing (where a homestead was retracting into a sculpture of toppled, weathered-grey boards), then ventured directly through the trees (where raccoons cavorted like kittens), one would land on the sandy lip of a spring-fed lake.

My new yard was perfectly private. It boasted a lawn as plush and green and, dare I say it — as *consummate* — as any

I'd ever seen. I pictured bocce ball parties, badminton games, swank weddings on this luxurious grass. I cartwheeled, practised sun salutes, and parked lounge chairs upon it. I tracked hours through the shadows that wheeled across its expanse.

But I also became positively obsessed with keeping the grass weed-free, and lost many an afternoon — all right, I lost entire livelong days — on hands and knees, meticulously combing through the blades and tweezing out junior dandelions, caragana, and creeping charlie the moment they dared to sprout.

We had everything before us...

The lawn was nothing less than a 5200-square-foot carpet fit for the queen, should she visit, and I was, despite my previous prejudice, in sweet, herbaceous love.

We had nothing before us...

Disparate as they were, I was passionate about both of my gardens. The few who knew each wondered at the irony: my city property was country-style; my country yard manicured to classic, French garden perfection.

Why? Perhaps the overgrown and chameleon inner-city garden landscape nourished the part of me that required short-term escape from my rush-hour life, even if it did, in fact, physically emulate it. An off-echo? Some weird psychological parallelism with a horticultural twist?

We were all going direct to Heaven, we were all going direct the other way...

My manicured country yard and encompassing woods acted as an exhalation, feeding me with both simpler and wilder fruits, so that I might have the fortitude to return to that other world (of round-the-clock cacophonies, responsibilities, and draining demands). Or at least that's about as much sense as I can muster from it. All I really know is that it was a fine balance indeed... *In short, the period was so far like the present period* ... and critical, and my heart amid the variegated greens and multifarious blossoms was ever a happier bird.

ALMOST EVE

YOUR NIGHT BREATH ON THE WINDOW LEAVES GHOSTS. The streetlight illumines a rectangle undusted with snow: where he is not parked. Downstairs, the new dog bawls as if even he already knows.

You remember the first time. Hardly dark; fervent voices compelled you to a commotion in the front yard. Your boy on all fours, head over an ice cream pail. Like an animal. His friends scattered when you burst between the houses, surprising yourself more than them: *What the fuck is going on here?*

The summer between grades eight and nine. The beginning, and long ago.

How well you know the window now. The waiting, the cliché. You are told this is something he will grow out of, like all those running shoes, every winter coat passed on to younger cousins. At his age you were on the verge of becoming his mother.

And sometimes he blames you.

What you have never told him: you love him better than anyone.

His sister, in at midnight, told you she saw him. Drunk and trying to pick a fight.

You understand what is happening here, know the emotional cocktail he can neither articulate nor subjugate is an inheritance: your grandfather, great-uncles, your cousin. You.

The pup wants to play at 4:13 a.m. You are awake anyway, a prayer forming itself between pillow and window because the next phone call will be a hospital; because he is barely alive; because he has been beaten and abandoned on a winter road; because he's slammed his car into unforgiving brick; because he's been stabbed by gang recruits; because a witness saw him jump off the Broadway Bridge; because the doctor wants to know if you'd like to hear what's in your son's crumpled note that says not enough but is right up-to-date with a sidebar confession: he knew where the dog had left messes and he hadn't cleaned them up.

Books you could fill with the waiting you've done, and it makes no sense. Your husband sleeps, though last night it was he who got up with the dog, found your firstborn passed out in a fetal position on the kitchen floor, reeking from his latest binge.

The boy sleeps in his jeans. His jacket. Sometimes he crashes into bed, sometimes it's the couch, the back step. He sleeps until 1:00 p.m., 4:00 p.m. He is too thin, his face a topography of acne, hands and arms a battlefield of scars. Of course there have been drugs, but you believe him when he says he is finished with that; he did not like what they made him think about.

In this house we are women who write letters when nothing else makes sense. Letters to him in grade eleven, grade twelve. 2003. Among the under-bed skin mags and refuse, rolled pages of his sister's handwritten lines, your own single-spaced type. Strategies employed to save he who will not be saved.

When he was eighteen, the two of you sat by a campfire at Cypress Hills. You spoke deep into the night, surrounded by lodgepole pines. A satellite of spent sunflower seeds spelled a story around your feet. He was about to enter the Canadian government's Katimavik program for youth — a nine-month commitment — and you had to know who you were saying goodbye to. You caught a glimpse, fleeting as the bull moose the two of you beheld in a clearing the next morning, transitory as the snow powdering your separate tents when you awoke.

Last October, you returned after two months in Europe. That first night he came home at 5:00 a.m. and you sat together, knees touching in the lamp-lit room. He told you how proud he was; wanted to hear about backpacking adventures; about your retreat in a Scottish castle. He wanted to talk about the big world. His beautiful hands were like birds, his voice a different tenor — slower, delivered with a philosophical edge — and for hours you believed this was the good and contemplative adult he had grown into.

You forgave the hour. The next day rose and fell. At 8:00 a.m. he stumbled to the couch. Drunk, or high. You'd been duped.

At 5:06 a.m. the pup is locked back into his kennel. Tea time, and while you wait for the storm that is a kettle set to boil, you spy a book in a bag at the back door, where it seems impossible. *I am a Bunny*. One of those sturdy board books for toddlers who would wreck any other kind. It tells a simple story:

I am a bunny. My name is Nicholas. I live in a hollow tree. In the spring, I like to pick flowers.

At two he knew all the words, could count to ten in four languages. At ten he wanted to be an entomologist. Six months ago he came home with swelling, bruises, and half a tooth. Sometimes the whole house smells of what he has become. He has told you, on this almost eve of his twenty-first birthday, that he never thought he'd live this long.

I chase the butterflies and the butterflies chase me.

You find a black marker, a white page. Tape *Your Mother Loves You Very Much* on the back door, where — if he comes home, if he can make out the letters — he will read it.

The puppy, a redbone coonhound, sleeps at long last. Before your son left this night, he peered into the dog's small, wrinkled mug and said: *Doesn't this little guy just cheer you up? Look at that face!*

More ghosts in the window. The double blur of headlights at the south end of the street.

Not him.

You are caught in the valley between packing his bags and whisking him out the door, and wanting to cocoon him in the softest blanket, rock him like you did so many nights through the early years.

I blow the dandelion seeds into the air.
To save him, and also to be exempted from having to.
Anything to know how to get this right.

SAN FRANCISCO

PHOTOS NOT TAKEN

Unphotographed:
A forty-two-year-old woman squatting on the Montgomery Station floor of the Bay Area Rapid Transit system, head down, chaotic locks worried through fingers. A backpack the size of a solid six-year-old stands at attention beside her on the concrete. Figures blur past in cross-directions, like digitally sped-up characters in a film featuring only movement and sound. She unfolds, returns to the ticket window. The orange-haired black woman repeats her words through the plexiglass: *Sorry, Hon, nothing yet.*

San Francisco's well into May and the season's uncharacteristically mild. The woman on the floor imagines a map, the kind one finds in shopping malls, envisions the heart-assuring: *You Are Here.* But where, exactly, is *here?* She's somewhere within the borders of a strange city in a country not her own, and everything important — money, credit and debit cards, glasses, meds, itinerary, tickets, digital camera, jewellery, make-up and maps — has continued down the subway track without her.

~

It was different from the beginning. I usually choose the destination, spend hours scouring Internet sites to learn what best to see and do — both on and off the beaten track — find the most reasonably priced and well-situated accommodation, including hostels and homestays.

This time: *I booked the flight to San Francisco.* T stood in my office doorway looking pleased, this man who had never booked a flight in his life, my husband of twenty years. *We leave May 29th.*

We hadn't even confirmed we were going; I was impressed. Perhaps my perpetual passion for adventure — perpetual lack of money be damned — was rubbing off.

Why San Francisco? You could say it was the Expedia.ca TV commercial: a man at a computer plans an anniversary trip to SF, then jump cuts of cable cars, the Golden Gate, seaside restaurants. You could say it was the movies we've seen, the reasonably low WestJet fare, a Toronto Blue Jays vs. Oakland A's game. You could call it timing. A whim.

~

A prairie gal flying into San Francisco is first amazed at the muscular green Marin Headlands, then the architecture of bridges. *There's the Golden Gate ... or is it the Bay Bridge?* The city seems to cling precariously to hills. Angel Island, Coit Tower and the neat rectangle of Golden Gate Park are easily distinguished.

In the airport I fed my card to the ATM and stuffed 300 greenbacks — always wanted to use that word — into my wallet, then we boarded Bay Area Rapid Transit, aka BART. No taxis for us: Type A and low-budget gal that I am, I'd copied a grid of the subway system, highlighted our routes and taped the whole business, along with detailed itinerary, myriad maps, prepaid tickets, and *Lonely Planet* discussion board tips, into my lifeblood coil-ringed binder.

On the subway beside us, a ship captain was returning from Nigeria. *If you come back to California next year, you should call.* He extended his business card with a manicured hand. *We're in the valley … forty-five minutes from the city.*

How generous. How *welcoming*, these San Franciscans.

We bustled through the doors at our stop, double-timed the stairs to the station. I turned to my husband, said: *This is too easy.*

Careful, Shell … you're going to jinx us.

Three minutes later I'm a-squat on a subway station floor, minus small backpack, and devoid of a single flipping clue.

~

When a Type A loses her coil-ringed binder in a reasonably large American city, the *caca* hits the proverbial fan. Where the heehaw were we? Was someone racking up my Visa as we spoke? By what miracle would we even find our hostel? I had a hazy idea from scrutinizing maps for weeks before the trip: north?

We started toward what I hoped was the North Beach district. And nothing mattered: not the iridescent sunshine reflected in windows and sunglasses, not the wildly gesticulating street people, the TransAmerica Pyramid, the pain between my shoulders from the oppressive pack, Chinatown's frenetic vegetable and souvenir markets, or the string of strip clubs and sex shops within which we found our inconspicuous hostel.

I shared my plight with the distracted young hostel employee, then stormed the phone, cancelling like crazy. Beyond a flight of single-lane stairs and a serpentine hall, our prebooked private room awaited: a one-body bed, a wall-bolted television, and a spectacular view of the vagrants shooting up in the alley's shadows.

I dumped the bag I'd managed *not* to forget on the subway, and my stomach decided it was well past dinner. My husband, fortunately, had *his* money and credit card. Married twenty years, yes, but our money remained strictly our own.

T, you're not going to let me starve, eh?

We sat in a Mexican restaurant beneath a blaring televised soccer game. Latinos roared at the set. I ordered two whopping burritos for myself and chased them with a Dos Equis beer. Exhausted and deflated, we returned to our room. After I pinched out my contact lenses, I slid my husband's glasses on; the prescription was several degrees off. I hadn't yet been to Lawrence Ferlinghetti's famous City Lights Bookstore, or the bars haunted by the beatnik poets, nor had I stepped back in time to the tie-dyed Haight-Ashbury district, but, Baby, everything already looked groovy to me.

~

I love to walk; my husband would rather do anything else. So we compromised, first walking along the Embarcadero, to Union Square, the Presidio, Pacific Heights, Russian Hill, back downtown, and around. Then we rented bikes and cycled along the marina, across the wind-swept Golden Gate, into the Marin Headlands, back to China Beach, up the insanely steep backside of Lombard. We rode the brakes down hairpin curves on the opposite side.

And something happened. In the short expanse of two days, I — neurotic, high-stressed drama queen that I can occasionally be — completely forgot about losing my backpack and everything important, and realized I was having a damn good time.

~

I dig research. The Internet, travel guides and library DVDs all play a part in trip planning. In one DVD I'd learned about a four-hour walking tour of the Castro district — the renowned gay area — led by a silver-haired woman named Trevor. It looked fabulous: fun and educational. I'd e-mailed Trevor and reserved a spot, never guessing that those four hours spent with complete strangers as we listened to anecdotes about the Castro's history would be the ultimate among a whole week of highlights in the city by the bay.

T and I enjoyed the long journey on foot from our hostel. The sun blasted our shoulders. A dreadlocked barista said we'd hit the city just right — after the rain and before the fog. We met Trevor and the other participants,

all female — two couples from England and cousins from
Puerto Rico and Silicon Valley — on the corner of Castro
and Market Street beneath the gargantuan rainbow flag.

These are the gayest four corners in the world, Trevor
began.

She seemed to know just about everyone in the district.
Many stopped to embrace her as we passed storefronts, like
the card shop, Does Your Mother Know, and a hardware/
craft store that she claimed sold *boas by the yard*. She told
us the history of activist Harvey Milk's assassination (she
had known him), discussed the rise of AIDS, and generously
shared her personal story. We sat entranced in the fenced
garden kept by the Noe Valley lesbians, and hung on every
witty word.

There was lunch. Trevor had surreptitiously ordered
an oversized anniversary dessert for us and we passed
out the forks. At the end there were hugs all around, and
coupons for gay-owned bars and businesses. At a pet shop
we bought a squeaky toy — a George Bush head — for our
dog, then carried on to the Mission District, which was so
reminiscent of our wanderings through Mexico, Venezuela
and the Dominican Republic, we were delightfully
transported.

But hey, we still had that two-for-one coupon for a bar,
called The Bar, in the Castro. Should we go? Why not?

The Bar was tunnel-ish, dusky. The music was 1970s
classic rock, and the bartender was knockdown, drag-out
gorgeous. There were seats along the bar and perhaps eight
other tables. It might have been 3:00 p.m. We ordered
drinks — fancy concoctions we'd never drink at home — and

settled in. How extraordinary we felt. How exhilarating to be in this hyper-friendly, super diverse American city, with its drag queens and druggies, its millionaires and movie stars, and simple folks just like us.

One table over, an old queen was getting seriously sloshed. He'd been shopping, he told us, and held up four bulging bags. At the bar, an accountant type was hitting on a guy with rockabilly hair. Two men breezed in with their dogs — a pair of sleek boxers — and, dog lover that I am, I slid off my seat to meet them.

More drinks, more laughs. Fewer inhibitions.

Rockabilly keeps looking at you, I whispered to T.

I know.

He's not even listening to that accountant guy.

I know.

I think he's going to come talk to us.

And he did, and we spent the next several hours conversing, toasting, and laughing ourselves stupid with Michael-the-Stylist, from Chicago. He'd dyed Gary Sinise's eyebrows and worked on Faye Dunaway's lips. He was hip, hilarious, and nearly as drunk as us.

~

Unphotographed:

Neon, night. A couple unhurrying down a street lined with strip clubs and stumblers. A burly, black bouncer calls: *Come on in, we'll have a threesome.* The woman is so surprised she explodes into laughter, as does the bouncer. Even her husband cracks what might be a smile.

⁓

We decided to do something else we'd never done: rent a car. Candyheart red, sporty, sunroof and all. We felt young, the car subtracting years off our lives. We felt in disguise.

This could be trouble, my husband said. The traffic was daunting: plus there's these outrageous hills, cable cars, the tricks one-way streets are known to play. My driver's licence was MIA with my wallet; at least *I* was spared. *Here goes nothing, S. You're navigating. Which way to the bridge?*

I needed bifocals. Map was in my lap, and I couldn't make sense of it. We were lost inside of five minutes. *Follow the car in front of you!*

What? T was fairly screaming.

So was I. *Just follow it! At least you won't go down a one-way street.*

We tailed, figure-eighted, doubled back, and eventually wound our way to the urban perimeter, across the Golden Gate Bridge, past the turn-off for Sausalito and north. We missed our exit for Muir Woods, and thus made our second destination our first.

Stinson Beach is an impeccable stretch of sand that fronts a great white shark breeding ground. The tide laps toward a rhyme of black rocks at one end of the beach. The word on my tongue was *moonscape.*

⁓

Unphotographed:
A woman kicks off her Nikes and cartwheels end over end across the wet slap of sand. She culls stones and pockets

shells, arranges them to spell her new favourite word, the quadra-syllabic *California*. She orders Neapolitan ice cream from a seaside vendor, feels like Betty or Veronica.

~

We drove to a lighthouse — closed — and to beaches where there was no one, just the knowledge of a fault-line a few legions beneath the water, and that merriest of widows, the wind.

The goal was to make it all the way up to Mendocino, hit clothing-optional Orr Hot Springs, then double back through Napa Valley before checking into our Marin Headlands Hostel. We did not succeed: places on the map are always further than they appear, and switchbacks make for leisurely going.

We eventually did find Muir Woods — redwoods you can drive through — and chose a trail that promised an ocean view. We hiked uphill and bloody forever. It must have been the air: we got silly, hugged and humped trees. There was no ocean view, just a rock-lounging lizard and the ubiquitous broken beer bottle on a highway's gravelled edge.

~

Unphotographed:
Rodeo Beach. A man witnesses two fisherman accidentally hook a gull. A woman scrambles up hills for the best lookout over the turbulent water. Spots a rookery of seals. Or rocks.

~

We went wine tasting in the Sonoma Valley. We had no idea about wine, didn't even know for certain how to properly hold a glass. The people at the wineries were good. Spotted Canadians and figured hockey talk was a sure bet. And it was. Ka-ching: we bought two bottles.

~

Unphotographed:
A couple sharing an anniversary dinner at a seaside restaurant in seriously upscale Sausalito. They don't get a window seat but it's two-for-one Tuesday, so they can't — and don't — complain.

Unphotographed:
A couple checking into their third hostel, at the far end of Fisherman's Wharf. If they hang out the window and squint just right, that blue scrap between barracks is the ocean.

Unphotographed:
A couple wearing headphones, touring Alcatraz. There's a convocation of black-crowned night herons and a ghost-watch of western gulls. No more Al Capone or "Doc" Barker, not a whiff of "Machine Gun" Kelly. The whole deal's smaller than she expected.

Unphotographed:
Leopard and angel sharks surrealistically swim over the heads of a couple who are moved through the aquarium on a conveyer belt.

Unphotographed:
Nine a.m., and a couple is ambling through Haight-Ashbury, second-guessing souvenirs for their teenagers. They buy a T-shirt with an open-armed, thumbs-up Jesus, delivering the vernacular *Wazzz Up?* A drunk Glaswegian bellybucks the husband. Everything's meant in good fun.

Unphotographed:
A woman circumnavigates Washington Park. Across from the cathedral where Joe DiMaggio and Marilyn Monroe posed for wedding photos, Chinese folks practise morning tai chi. Performance poetry, the woman thinks.

Unphotographed:
Evening, and a couple is cradled in the bleachers at McAfee Coliseum; the Blue Jays take on the Oakland A's. They spend a minor fortune on peanuts and sing "Take Me Out to the Ball Game." This does not even feel ridiculous.

Unphotographed:
A couple on a red cable car. She's squashed between strangers in the back, he's dangling off the front. If the brakes fail on this thing they'll rocket into the bay, perhaps land near the basking sea lions.

Unphotographed:
A guy on a subway who's had better decades. Today he can't believe his freaking luck. Three hundred dollars. Sweet.

They are twenty years married, sometimes happy, sometimes not. In two years there will be unfathomable heartbreak and divisions, but currently they're living the commercial, and they know it.

BLUE HAWAII

MY HUSBAND AND I ARE IN THE ALOHA STATE. WE'RE not here to commemorate a birthday; there's been no windfall of any kind. We're here terminating a twenty-two-year marriage which outsiders have long thought blissful, and, for the most part, they've bloody well been spot on. Even during our nine-month separation in 1992–1993 (during which T moved out, my FM-radio-voiced lover moved in, and the kids zoomed back and forth between Dad's place and home) we behaved exemplarily toward each other. Partnered with our new partners, we once had a doubles tennis match; it was all so goddamn civilized. Now our children are adults, and we have also grown into people we don't always recognize.

We are trying to choreograph the consummate separation, right down to matching responses when people ask why we've split:

Me: *We really like each other, but we've started to bicker* —
Him: Bicker, *or fight?*

Me: *Um,* bicker, *over the last several years, and as we'll always be a major part of each other's lives* —

Him: *Because of the kids?*

Me: *Yes, because of the kids… we want to end the formal relationship before we begin to hate each other. How does* that sound?

He doesn't name family and friends' most probable responses — *Have you tried counselling? Any hope of reconciliation?* — and neither do I. Each would require another prepared statement, and we're too tired to engineer answers for every query we're destined to get.

Although the backpacks are getting heavier each year — at least for my osteoporotic bones — we sausaged them full of summer clothes and snorkelling gear and set out for Hawaii like nineteen-year-olds on spring break, though of course *our* spring break is something altogether different.

We have been in Hawaii nine days — five nights on Oahu, Maui for three — and now we're back where we began, staying at the Seaside Hostel in Honolulu, with just a few sleeps left. Aloha.

Aloha, the most common word in the Hawaiian language and used interchangeably (and universally) as *Hello* and *Goodbye,* comes from *Alo,* meaning *presence, front, face* or *share,* and *ha,* meaning *breath.* A presence of breath. In ancient times — and, as I've read but never witnessed, still today — Hawaiians put their foreheads together and say *alo,* and then breathe out saying *ha,* thus literally exchanging life's breath.

Currently I am on the beach at Waikiki. The weather is that lethal combination of hotter-than-Hades and windy as well, and I'm already sun-stroked. For the previous two hours I hung out with the oscillating fan in our room. Now I've found the beach's sole scrap of shade: at the base of a lava wall, beside a Japanese woman in long pants and a formidable sun hat. I've brought a novel to the waterfront, a good one, purchased last summer on one of our trips to Seattle or Portland, but I can't concentrate enough to give it the close read it deserves.

As a fellow bus passenger remarked on the ride to Waimanalo Bay: *Honolulu is Calgary with a beach*. Well, that's one way of unromanticizing it, but we've done both sea *and* city holidays before, and consider this a two-birds, one-stone arrangement. At the Seaside Hostel, two blocks from the waves, we are fairly surrounded by bars — including Angles, the nearly-next-door gay bar we frequent — and all-hour people and traffic. Last night I was certain I heard a gunshot. Girls were screaming, guys trumpeting their bravado. Same old music. Still, we enjoy the intimate hostel, the strangers we've come to call friends: Colleen, a forty-five-year-old waitress from San Francisco, who is passionate about surfing and sports a board-generated goose egg between her long-lashed eyes; Leon, a free spirit in his late fifties, who gives us friendship bracelets in ocean colours, made while "in recovery" in southeast Asia; Dieter, a grandfather from Humboldt, Germany, whom I caught naked-by-surprise on our first night; and Andrew, a twenty-two-year-old Tasmanian, who's been travelling for the last year and has twenty-five different stamps on his passport. Add an assortment of Aussies and Brits and a Brazilian with whom we played Texas Hold 'Em, add the hostel's laid-back American staff, and there's the happy snap of our scene.

Looming separation aside, the trip has now taken on the familiar, melancholic air of yet another much-enjoyed vacation fast approaching its end. T says that of all our trips, this has been his favourite. Despite laughable finances (a kid working part-time at a gas station would earn thousands more than me), it seems we've lived our lives from holiday to holiday. And T's right: this has been a gooder.

I didn't expect it. This is, after all, Hawaii. Not exactly exotic. No foreign language to navigate, no funky currency, and there's an ABC store on almost every corner. Polynesian culture is enchanting — we find ourselves *mahalo*-ing within two days — but we were fools to pay $200 US for a luau in Lahaina, even if it was "the most authentic on the islands."

Although I'd anticipated great snorkelling at the Hanauma Bay Nature Preserve, I never imagined I'd make the acquaintance of a green sea turtle while deep-diving off the northwest coast of Maui all on my lonesome. I did not leave home with any intention of surfing, nor imagine I would actually catch a wave within my first few attempts. (Beginner's luck: I was on the water three hours, all told, and caught exactly four waves. Still, what a freaking rush.)

The best parts, however, have been my hours alone. Each morning I tiptoe out the door past my hostel-mates, just as the sun starts pitching light on the monolithic beachfront hotels. Then: I run like hell.

I run along Kuhio Beach, past the police station (housed in the surfer-named Duke Paoa Kahanamoku Building), down Kalakaua's winding walkway, past birds-of-paradise, frangipani and orchids, past the lei-graced statue of Duke Kahanamoku, past a mastiff (also wearing a lei), past a pavilion which will later fill with chess players, past the hula mound, where a free show is staged daily at 6:30 p.m., past beach volleyball nets, past Queens Beach, then Sans Souci. I wind through both high- and low-end residential areas; through Kapiʻolani Park; and Ala Moana State Recreation Area, where the homeless sleep within banyan vines. I chug up Diamond Head, then down along the Ala Wai Canal or into the business section of Honolulu. I race around Magic Island, on top of my game, heart bursting not from exertion but from the raw thrill of being outdoors, and physically strong, and solitarily exploring, as full of primal energy as I've ever been. I average two sweat-soaked hours a day before T's even considered rising for the hostel's free coffee and toast.

(*This is not a criticism, Dear, only fact. You're laid-back, God love you, and I've never learned how to relax.*)

This is some of what's wrong with us.

At this moment I am trying to determine which figure on the water is my soon-to-be-estranged husband. If I were closer it would be easy. A few days ago we stripped off at Little Beach, the nude beach on Maui's south shore, next to Big Beach, near Makena. The all-over tanned were skinny fishing, playing skinny Frisbee, and enjoying skinny almost everything else. They were shaved or not, circumcised or not, young or not. T had the best body on the beach by a country mile. (Or a city mile, depending on how you measure.) Even the jockish guys were checking him out. I wonder what it's like to be that comfortable in one's own skin. Oh, I was bare, too, but painfully conscious of it. From behind, I look like a broad-shouldered fourteen-year-old boy. Well, we're athletes, eh? Good at things that have to do with strength and water. I'll go with that.

Although all of Hawaii has been kind to us, Maui knocked the shorts off Oahu. You can drive from shore to shore on the freewayless island and be out-and-out ecstatic to do it. Driving the coastline was a blast: the sporty rental car, other drivers giving us the "hang loose" sign, Jawaiian reggae broadcast via a radio station in Japan.

The twisty, jungle-edged "Road to Hana" sparked Cape Breton déjà vu. We consumed a fabulous meal (crab and steak) at Jacques in Paia — a sugar cane plantation town turned world-class surfing/windsurfing destination, with Buddhist temples, and an organic grocery store where I couldn't even buy a Diet Coke. I saw actor Owen Wilson in that store. And the kid on the till was from Burnaby. I loved the six warning signs before the black sand beach at Pa`iloa Bay in Wai`napanapa State Park: *Dangerous Shorebreak; Strong Current; Man-O-War; Jellyfish; Waves Break On Ledge;* and the ubiquitous *No Lifeguard On Duty, Swim At Your Own Risk.*

We stayed at the Tropohouse B & B, in rural Haiku (poet that I've sometimes tried to be, how could we not?), where we slept on the top floor of a cedar-walled A-frame, woke each morning to cock-a-doodle-dos, and forgot our leis (from the outrageously overpriced luau — clearly, I'll never get over this) in the mini-fridge.

In the capital city of Lahaina, one of the world's largest banyan trees creates a natural, shade-streaked venue under which island artists and craftspeople sell their wares. A congregation of neo-hippies sprawled in the park near the library, passing around Maui-Wowie. Behind me, on a cell-phone, a long-legged feller in designer-slashed jeans and thousand-dollar shades:

Hi, this is Derek Rothchild. I'm at my house in Maui, but I'll be back in Switzerland next week...

I can recommend happy hour at The Blue Lagoon in Lahaina. I recommend happy hour at Life's A Beach in Kihei. Happy hour anywhere in Paia.

Ah, Maui. What a fabulous run on your shores, too.

Back on Oahu I stare into the waves, far beyond the bobbing heads of children and idle splashers, to where approximately seventy surfers await the next swell. They are all same-shaped, one colour. Which one is he? I have no idea.

So I wait.

Three hours now. T has still not paddled in, nor have I spotted him. It really burns my hibiscus.

A light rain falls — what locals apparently refer to as pineapple juice — and fickle tourists abandon the beach en masse. Beyond the surfers: cruise ships with higher populations than most of the towns I've lived in. A sailboat with a striped blue and white mast: one triangle of bikini. Somewhere someone is playing reggae, and above it all, another jetliner brings more mainlanders to paradise.

They tell you perfection does not exist. They are wrong. There is so much of it here: the young women are flawless in bikinis, palm fronds postcard-pristine in their windy waving. So much to distract me from my job of ensuring that my partner-in-crisis is safe.

T, I don't know what colour your board is, whether it's a longboard or the more challenging short. Are you wearing a shirt? Sure wish I knew which of those figures, so many hundreds of metres away, belonged to you. I hope another surfer hasn't cracked you, that no shark has made a meal of your succulent legs. Will the storm cloud to the south bring you in?

I suppose I've always realized this, but it especially irks me during *this* vacation how most of us do exactly the same things with cameras. Parents shoot their kids building sandcastles. The sun's about to set and everyone snaps it on cue. All this robotic sameness is getting to me. In fact, anything that reeks of even the slightest tradition has really been getting beneath my sunburn. Is it my age? I'm a little young to be so crotchety.

What I'm mostly feeling is impatient. I humour T by accompanying him to the International Marketplace, and later, the Flea Market at the Football Stadium, but the glut of souvenirs is obscene to my ever-more-minimalist sensibility. At the flea market I'm spent after half an hour. I grab a slab of cement and tell T — who loves crowds and shopping — to retrieve me when he's done. He's gone a little lifetime, and I grow dizzy watching a pony-tailed vendor try to sell over-priced, wood-polished clocks in the shape of dolphins.

This is some of what's wrong with us.

Is that you, straddling a board in the line-up? I watch the corduroy swell lines, conscious even of the moments I need to blink, because if you've really caught onto this surfing thing, if you're *really* carving the waves now, doing a bottom turn just after you've dropped in, say, or performing cutbacks, you wouldn't want me to miss it, and nor would I. I don't profess to know anything about the sport — we did not bother with a lesson — except that it's mostly about timing. Mostly you wait. And when a reasonable wave is approaching, you paddle approximately five good strokes in the angle of the wave before it hits, then jump to a crouch (called the *pop-up*), then: Yee-haw.

Usually I was too late, or I botched my positioning and ended up in the soup. Often the big waves got the best of me, and I starfished through surf and sky. The real surfers call this *getting worked*.

Another catamaran glides through the surfers. A guy on the bow blows a conch as they near shore; 'tis a most effective horn.

My eyes hurt from all the staring across the water. Almost four hours now, my Japanese neighbour and her family long returned to whence they came.

On the horizon, veteran surfers are showing off. I spy with my salt-sore eyes two pairs of surfers doubling on one board each, and there, to the right … is that someone surfing upside-down? It is. Buddy's doing a handstand as he carves across a wave.

At Hanauma Bay we parked our towels beside a pair of Vancouverites, agreeing to take turns watching each other's cameras and gear so we could snorkel with our partners. Mostly the water is shallow, and despite the nine-minute video all are obliged to watch before entering this precarious reef, mostly people *do* crawl all over the coral.

Our kids would dig a day like this, but apparently it ain't fun for everyone. I overhear one podgy girl of about seven whine to her parents: *Why did we have to come here? My feet hurt, I'm cold, and I hate this!*

T and I swim out to where it's much deeper. The reef is like canyons, or what you might expect to see on the moon, and the current shoves us around, big time. I lose my veteran grandfather's monogrammed ring twice, and both times miraculously find it. Time two I dig it out near a razor-barbed urchin.

Ka'anapali Beach, Maui. This particular section, also known as Black Rock, offers outstanding views across the Auau Channel. Here is the apogee of our journey: parallel beach towels — twin blue lozenges on white sand — and the surprise of humpback whales while the machines of our hearts gear down, as if slowing will help us forget this business of division. Scanning the horizon for breaching whales is like watching fireworks; that kind of collective waiting, then the crowd goes *Ahh.* Behind the whales' intermittent black backs, larger humps that are the islands of Molokai and Lanai.

Again, best is when I'm alone, the ear-buds of T's iPod buried in my ears. He is in the water, trailing sea turtles, and I am listening to salsa from Cuba. This could be that country's sun, sand, wind licking hair across my sunglasses.

We take turns snorkelling here — no trusty Canadians to swap patrols with. Me, then him, me again, him. We are only five steps in with our flippers before the world drops away: palenose parrot fish; the achilles, yellow and sailfin tangs; eyestripe surgeon fish; raccoon butterfly fish, the mullets and the moorish idols, all in a geography where one might expect birds.

I love too much the deep. Is this my problem?

Far from shore I straight-dive down, see another green sea turtle beneath a rocky ledge. At this depth I hear whale-song. It's surreal — a radio station coming in badly — and utterly awesome.

T drips out of the water and one-ups me. Says: *You swam* behind *a turtle, I actually touched one.*

On the flight to Honolulu I made a friend. Casey-from-Williams-Lake, BC (age *almost thirteen*) and I chatted across the entire Pacific. More and more I've come to believe that I'm really an adolescent boy disguised as a middle-aged woman. I also made fast friends with Eustacia, at Angles. Twenty-eight and sporting a crimson mohawk, this engineer from Boulder was just returning from six months at the South Pole. We pounded back beer while T, the only straight bloke in the bar, participated in a pool tournament.

Eustacia: *So I've got to ask. Why does a straight couple hang out at a gay bar? In this country it's usually because they're looking for a woman to add to the mix …*

Me: *Um, we come here because we can't stand rednecks, and you're not likely to find many in a gay bar. Some of our best friends are gay. And gay bars are just, well … more fun.*

I don't know if she believes me, and I don't fan that fire by telling her we also spend many of our sunbathing hours at the aptly named Queens Beach. When T loses out in the High-Low final to Francine, a mute, blonde and DDD-cupped transvestite with collagen lips — she purses them to indicate her shots — I tell Eustacia that I'm an affectionate lass and give her a warm hug and kiss. She says she's an affectionate lass, too.

Rain-soaked and getting crankier. Where the hell is he?

I give up, give in, approach the lifeguards.

I believe my husband is out there but I haven't seen him for hours. This is not like him. I'm worried.

What does he look like?

Tall. Very muscular. He may have a shirt on.

The lifeguard scouts through his binoculars — I can't help but think of that Alex Colville painting, and *Baywatch*. The guard shrugs, then passes the glasses to me. They don't help one iota.

Ah, Miss? We're shutting down now. I'm sure he's just fine.

I leave the beach, wondering. Soon I'm climbing the stairs to the shop on Koa Avenue where we rent our boards.

Has my husband been here?

Yes, he came back about two hours ago.

Jesus. I don't know what happened. I could not have missed him, eyes pinned, as they were, and bloody-well burning now. My contact lenses feel like two ragged, miniature tin can lids.

I return to the hostel, and there he is. A fight, not a *bickering*, ensues.

I was sitting at exactly the spot we were at a few days ago, just like you said. I waited for four hours. In the rain. Where the hell were you?

I was at exactly the spot we were at a few days ago. You must have been in the wrong place.

I know I wasn't.

Had to have been.

We are both absolutely certain we are right. Again. This, too, is some of what's wrong with us.

Soon we will fly home, share laptop photos with friends. There will be a great bare-chested shot of T on a bike near Honolulu's Chinatown. A not-bad photo of me doing a cartwheel on Queens Beach, though I had to do it five times before T got the timing right. The cartwheel. Yes. Only my husband knows things like this about me: that I cartwheel on beaches, and write words in the sand the sea soon erases.

We are on the precipice now. The first words regarding our separation are about to be leaked, and, once uttered, the gears are in motion. I don't want to explain how we still hold hands, I still call him *Love*.

No one is going to *get* us.

Aloha is a way of living and treating each other with love and respect; it connotes a joyful and harmonious sharing of life. Honolulu-born Bette Midler uses it often. We heard it frequently between 1968 and 1980 on the TV crime drama *Hawaii Five-O*. The Aloha Spirit was what the last queen of Hawaii, Lili'uokalani, was writing about in the historically famous song, "Aloha 'Oe."

After all these years, I know little more of marriage than I do of surfing, but I think it does not get much better than parallel towels on a slate of white sand, humpback whales breaching while the mechanics of troubled hearts slow down.

Aloha, T. And aye, it's been a gooder, indeed.

HALEAKALA SUNRISE

IMPOSTERS, THAT'S WHAT WE ARE. A FRACTURED FAMILY pretending otherwise, and together we rise in a budget hotel room in Kihei, Maui, at 2:30 a.m.

The calendar has just rolled over into the Year of our Lord 2008. The mini-fridge is crammed with bottles of outrageously sweet drink mixes — piña colada, mai tai, strawberry daiquiri — and the requisite alcohol to ignite them. Father and twenty-three-year-old son, who purchased this saccharine cache, anticipated it would usher us into the new year. Collectively barefoot on the postcard beach, we'd toast the tropical moon and humpback whales while fireworks crayoned the sky, and firecrackers echoed against the fragile drums of our ears. The truth: we all fell asleep in the room during a Ben Stiller movie before the clock struck midnight, though T insists he *almost* stayed awake for the year-turning.

A few months earlier, when my bright, lovely, twenty-one-year-old daughter was furious with the world, most of her vitriol was aimed squarely at me. I was already donning a shawl of shame, heard the phantasmal whisperings of *There goes the Bad Mother Who Abandoned Her Children and Husband of Twenty-two Years* whenever I was in the city.

I rarely drove the one and a half hours to make the visit. E-mails from family were infrequent and unfriendly: *I hate this pretend family bullshit. Oh, let's go to Hawaii and be the Leedahl family for two weeks, then come back and disband and forget that we are family.* Strangers that we were inevitably becoming in the four months since I'd left, I wasn't sure we could pull this vacation off. It was mind-bending to consider that nine months earlier, T and I were on this very island wearing wedding rings.

Everyone was to have their bags packed and at the ready for this morning's pre-dawn adventure: a drive to the village of Haiku, where for US $370.58 (in total) the good folks at the Haleakala Bike Company (HBC) would transport us to the summit of the Haleakala Volcano, the largest dormant volcano on earth (boasting a crater 3000 feet deep, seven miles long, two miles wide, and twenty-one miles in circumference) in Haleakala National Park.

All of Manhattan could fit inside it.

We would watch the sun rise (if it did not prove too cloudy), then cycle back down to Haiku — approximately thirty miles — on Gary Fisher mountain bikes. We were into it. Sleep-deprived but adrenaline-jacked.

~

The drive from Kihei leads past the five-star, palm-lined resorts, the gracefully waving sugar cane fields, and the factory, in which we joke we'll all work after we quit our real lives, through the outskirts of Kahului and the airport, where Cyndi Lauper — in the plane seat behind me — did not disembark, and Logan befriended a spotted gecko whilst T and I debated how much rental car insurance to buy. It winds us along the windswept north coast and through our favourite hippie/surfer town, Paia. Further along the Hana Highway you come to the eleven-mile marker, aka the turn-off into Haiku.

"Did you bring your bathing suits?" I ask no one in particular. "We might hit a beach later."

One *yes*, one *no*, and one *I don't remember*. It really is too early to think.

~

There is one other occupied car in the parking lot at the Haiku Marketplace, an old cannery building-turned mall, and home of the HBC. It is as dark inside as it is out, and the door — I check — is locked.

"I've gotta take a piss," Logan announces, and exits to pee in the bird-of-paradise and hibiscus, away from the eye of a halogen lamp.

"At least it's not raining," T says.

"Well, at least not *yet*." I wouldn't claim the title of pessimist, but our vacation's suffered an inauspicious beginning. On Christmas day we fled winter in Saskatoon and endured a six-hour layover in Calgary. Next up: a three-hour weather- and mechanical-related delay — we were detained inside the airplane — at the Vancouver airport. Air Canada lost every ounce of my luggage, and one of Taylor's bags. The Seaside Hostel closed at midnight, and we'd be arriving at around 2:00 a.m., which necessitated frantic phone calls from a borrowed cell phone, and T and Logan shuttling away from the Honolulu Airport ahead of us. Mother and daughter brought up the rear in an interminable Lost Luggage report line, and claimed the survival package Air Canada provides in such circumstances: a mini tube of toothpaste; a folding toothbrush; a razor; a tablet of soap; a few squeezes of hand lotion; a strange, scalp-clawing brush; and an extra-large white T-shirt.

I was perhaps a little too excited about that T-shirt. Apart from the clothes on my back, it was all I possessed.

There was also the rain, cyclonic wind, the uncharacteristic cold. "This is the worst winter we've had in twenty years," one well-swaddled Hawaiian blithely informed me.

Fan*tas*tic. We paid all this money and we're not even going to get a tan.

~

Lights are burning inside the HBC now. We grab our bags, double-check that we've locked the rental car, and shuffle into a warehouse-like room. A Danny DeVito-sized employee is trying too hard to be funny; his efforts are lost on us.

We get down to business.

"Name?"

"Leedahl. Group of four."

He checks his list. "You're not on here."

My heart founders. We will never be able to repeat this early morning — or this vacation — together again. "But I have our receipt, and a confirmation number." Do I? Surely not on my person, but certainly somewhere.

"Well, let me check the computer. How do you spell that?"

I spell, he checks. "Ah, you're supposed to be here January 3rd, not today."

T and I exchange panicked glances. Whose fault was this?

"But that's okay, we can accommodate you."

Whew. We each sign the ubiquitous death and dismemberment waiver — not one of us reads it — and once the remaining twenty or so participants arrive, Danny DeVito individually fits us with helmets in a little stand-up comedy show involving encephalitic jokes. The helmets are serious, Darth Vader-type affairs. Taylor and I get a hell of a kick out of them. High-end hooded Columbia Sportswear rain/wind-suits (peacock blue for the boys; army green for the girls) and NASA-esque gloves are also distributed.

Logan's first to slide into the heavy pants. "What's this deal made of ... some kind of Gore-Tex? A guy could survive chemical warfare in this thing."

"I guess it gets cold up there," T says, snapping into his jacket, "but hey, at least it's not Saskatchewan."

This is a popular refrain.

We occupy an entire bench in front of the HBC while latecomers straggle in and are gear-attired. The group consists mostly of adults. There are a few couples, one family from Seattle —"We love Seattle!" I exclaim — and another American family, with super-sized, obnoxious kids. I ask the Seattle mother to take our photo. Another group employs me to take theirs.

"Fuck, it's early," Logan says. And it is. Still dark. All of 3:30 a.m. now.

Another employee arrives. Lanky, thin-armed, long greasy tangle of almost-black hair: exquisite. And is that a French Canadian accent? He reminds me of a bike courier. Also a very hot, slightly aggravated (there are too many people for one bus, and the van's not working so well) Jesus Christ.

The group is split between drivers DeVito and Jesus. I nudge my family toward the Divine.

Exceptional choice. Once our host swings behind the wheel and secures the door, he launches into witty, articulate, and educational anecdotes about the area, the activity, and his own life. Born in Belgium (or Belarus — I've flipped my hood up and hearing's impeded), he's lived all over the globe, including Montreal — T says, "Good guess on the accent, Shell" — and Detroit, which he left after the second time he was car-jacked. He relays some of the stupid questions tourists have posed on this excursion, including: "How long is the drive to the mainland?" "Can you swim beneath the island?" and "Is the volcano down all the way?"

We learn that in Hawaiian folklore, Haleakala's hollow was home to the grandmother of the demigod Maui. According to legend, Maui's grandmother helped him lasso the sun and force it to slow its journey across the sky, "in order to lengthen the day."

A regular fountain of knowledge is our Jesus. He explains that at the highest elevations, the alpine/aeolian zone appears barren. "Rainfall quickly sinks into the porous, rocky land, so few plant species can establish seedlings." The exceptions are a few hardy shrubs, grasses, and a blooming plant he's particularly enthusiastic about, the rare silversword (*ahinahina*). "It grows nowhere else in the world, lives from about fifteen to fifty years, blooms only once — shooting up a five- or six-foot stalk — then bites it." He identifies silversword on the roadside as we pass, but night obscures it from mine eyes.

I'm also interested to hear about the Baldwins — "Not the movie star Baldwins, but the Maui Baldwins" — a famous entrepreneurial and agricultural family which, Jesus explains, has ranched on Maui for six generations, and apparently owns more than half the island's land; perhaps up to ninety percent of the resorts, golf courses, and ranches, as well as the Hui No'eau Visual Arts Center in Makawao. They have an avenue, a beach park, and a high school named after them, and are responsible for Maui's pineapple industry. If that isn't enough, they're also the Baldwin Piano people, and Henry Baldwin, known as "Father Maui," developed (with partner Samuel Alexander) the Hamakua Ditch System, which provides water from East Maui's rainforest to Central Maui's sugar cane fields. (Oh, and the Baldwins own the factory where we'll one day work, too.) Jesus tells us that when the family donated a portion of their land for Haleakala National Park, they were given the rights to supply all the beef to the military.

"Gotta get me a Baldwin," he jokes. "Preferably one in her twenties."

He shares tales about directionally challenged cyclists he's recovered on this tour — he eventually found one kid at the Kahului harbour — and asks us to memorize a map by repeating after him: *Right turn out of the park; turn right at the next two forks; hang a left at the stop sign; a right at Makawao; then a left at Kokomo Road. Cycle past the ATM sign in Haiku and turn into the mall.* Home free.

One passenger says she heard about a ban on these volcano bike tours. I'd heard about it, too. I'd read online that in October 2007, the superintendent of Haleakala National Park called for an emergency, minimum sixty-day "Safety Stand-Down" of all commercial downhill bike tours in the park. Last year several serious accidents and three fatalities occurred on tours offered by companies that advertise a "guided" experience, and five of those seven downhill bike companies — although not HBC, thank you, Jesus — can no longer operate in the park. The controversial stand-down has had a trickle-down effect on Maui's tourism industry. It's still under review.

Jesus concludes his commentary and concentrates on the winding road. It's black as an oil spill out there; we could be anywhere. My body slides into T's as we round hairpin curves. He doesn't mind; we're not *that kind* of exes.

Everything's surreal: blindly winding up the steep incline; this bomb-squad costume; the helmet, heavy as a fish bowl on my lap. Our kids — who are no longer kids — are sitting bolt upright ahead of us. Both are asleep. And suddenly, one row behind and across, a woman begins to weep. It's almost a pleasant chirping at first. I turn, see that her boyfriend has her head tucked into his chest, bird-like. Her shoulders are heaving. And then she really gets into it. Blatant bawling, like a child in a grocery store who just doesn't care.

The chap from Seattle, beside me, turns and politely asks: "Is she okay?"

"No," the boyfriend snaps. "She's *not* okay."

There are ways to be and ways not to be. You don't call anyone after 10:30 p.m. (and in some circles, even 10:00 is iffy) unless it's a lover or an emergency. If someone has one or two items in the grocery queue behind you and you have thirty-six, you let him or her through. When a stranger graciously enquires after the well-being of your mate, you do not snap. What an extraordinary ass; I turn red on Seattle's behalf. And what's up with the blubbering girlfriend, anyway? Is it the twenty-nine switchback curves within the last ten miles? The drastically increasing cold? The three recent fatalities? Suck it up, sistah. Y'all signed up for this.

~

We arrive at the summit. As disoriented as I am in the solid dark, I identify the washroom and hightail toward it. It's huge, and ubiquitously National Park-ish. (Think Banff, or Waskesiu.)

The temperature is positively lunar. There are other sunrise spectator hopefuls milling about — non-cyclists — wearing toques and gripping thermoses. All manner of quilts mummify their bodies. *Smart* people. Or at least experienced. There are photographers with telephoto lenses that may well cost more than my car. The greatest surprise is that this number of people are conscious at this ungodly hour, and submitting themselves to this unholy temperature for something that's not even a sure bet. (Clouds may obscure the epiphanic moment.)

To get the best view, one must climb to the crater's rim. It's treacherous. Bat's-wing-black; no clear-cut path; and thousands of jagged lava rocks of all sizes stud the course. Plus, we're in a hurry, not wanting, after everything, to miscue by a few minutes and miss out on the waking sun. I lead the way, the family clomping up behind me, and succeed in scraping the hell out of my knee on a rock that's leapt out and bit. It's a mystery how I don't rip the Columbia pants but do tear my skin.

From what we can vaguely discern, it's awesome inside the crater: deeply sculpted, and richly coloured with red, black, yellow and green cinder dust and ash. Volcanic vents, rocky peaks, cinder cones and small depressions make for an alienscape. Sci-fi movies have been filmed here. And *Total Recall*. Numerous other movies and TV programs I'm too bone-cold to remember the names of. We huddle, and ask a French couple: *s'il vous plaît* take our photo?

"Shell, take a shot of the crater," T says. He points at two distant peaks. "Get one of Mauna Loa and Mauna Kea … two of the five Big Island volcanoes."

I do and do, but nothing turns out. The sky is variegated blues above cloud cover, and the flash doesn't do anything justice.

~

Ten minutes, twenty-five. I suck at waiting. When's the freaking sun going to show? I'm shivering like I haven't since I was a kid on a snowmobile in northern Saskatchewan. Frozen fingers, ears. It took hours of register-sitting to thaw my feet. I'm tempted to say *Screw the sunrise, I'll meet you back on the bus*, but then up she rises: a tease of lemon-orange, then smouldering-coal light against an igneous silhouette.

A reverent silence has descended upon the crowd. No one moves. Nothing and everything is happening. I am reminded of Annie Dillard's account of another phenomenon, the viewing of an eclipse: "It looked as though we had all gathered on hilltops to pray for the world on its last day." This *feels* like the last day. Or the first.

Mark Twain described the Haleakala sunrise as "... the sublimest spectacle" he ever witnessed. True, as Logan says, "A sunrise is a sunrise" — and, truth be told, they're pretty damn special out my own east windows in rural Saskatchewan — but I am distinctly aware that this, here, with the four of us, is a spectacle of never-again.

But oh, the obnoxious cold. Before the light show is even halfway wrapped up, I'm heading back down the slope. As Dillard also stated in that "Total Eclipse" essay: "But enough is enough. One turns at last even from glory itself with a sigh of relief. From the depths of mystery, and even from the heights of splendor, we bounce back and hurry for the latitudes of home."

Dusky light now, and no more rattler rocks.

"Right behind you, Mamacita," Taylor says, and her big brother and father are on her heels.

We board the bus. Our inordinately attractive driver takes a head count. Where's the super-sized family? Someone volunteers to search. We wait an extra twenty minutes. Jesus is perturbed.

One does not cycle from the peak — er, crater — of Haleakala. A trailer containing the rental bikes has been left at a "stage" some 6,500 feet above the base, and it is here that we mount our steeds. Jesus prompts us to make the "hang loose" sign — we feel ridiculous — and he takes our family photo.

"Could be worse," Logan says. "We could be wearing leis."

We tip Jesus well.

Keep to the right and *Let all vehicles pass* are the only rules, and they're cardinal. Taylor's off, and Logan, too. T waits for me to wrangle the digital camera back into the waterproof backpack. Now we're away.

Lordy, it's steep, and exhilarating as all get-out. But what's this already? Several disobedient cyclists in the centre of the road. This makes T — a serious cyclist — crazy, and he hollers at them to get over.

The kids are soon miles below us. We've made a plan: if we get separated — and we will — we'll meet at the left turn-off after the two right-turn forks. We'll have lunch in Makawao: a *paniolo*, or cowboy town, with boutiques and art galleries, and — Jesus promised — a fabulous Mexican restaurant.

God, but it's grand, rocketing down the side of a volcano in January on a sturdy bike, wind tearing at my eyes and ears. Where a bluff of fragrant pines bracket the road, I'm reminded of a Gulf Islands cycling trip. Where the ocean is glimpsed far below us and I can see forever, I recall Cape Breton's Cabot Trail. It's always like this when I travel now: every landscape fuels memories of another.

But Maui is all its own, too. Surprisingly rural in these heights. Lush sweeps of yellow-green grass, wood thickets, horse barns, corrals. Subalpine shrub-land covers extensive areas below the alpine/aeolian zone and above the forest line. The shrubs sustain a variety of Hawaii's bird species, including the nene, the wild Hawaiian goose that shares its ancestry with the Canada goose.

Such extraordinarily diverse vegetation within the zones: the forest canopy's dominated by ohi à ài trees in the higher elevations, grading into a mixed ohi à ài and koa canopy at lower levels. Smaller trees, ferns, shrubs, and herbs appear in the "understory." Animals, grass invasions, and fire have conspired to drastically reduce the dry forests; small patches have been preserved in Kaupo Gap.

When we whiz past grazing horses and dilapidated outbuildings, I feel like I've been transported into an old western, but I'm also in a Mexican movie, and *The Sound of Music*.

Below 4,000 feet, we come to "upcountry Maui," with its market gardens, lodges, galleries, and Kula botanical gardens. If one has the time and desire, one might explore Keokea, the Chinese community, the Tedeschi Winery, the Enchanted Gardens, or a beach.

We've been warned that we'll likely encounter rain on this adventure, and we do. Rainforest occupies the windward slopes of Haleakala: annual rainfall ranges from 120 inches to 400 inches. The dry forest zone, on the leeward slopes, sees 20 to 60 inches.

"This frickin' rain is not very funny." I know that T, behind me, can't hear.

The road is salamander slick: it would take little — the slightest tap from a car's bumper — and we'd be punted over the ineffectual rail into oblivion. But what a rush. And tight curves.

Obedient biker that I am, I follow the rules and cycle on the extreme right edge … where eventually my front tire catches loose gravel … and I begin to fishtail at an alarming speed. Losing control. My handlebars jackknife and I'm pitched, still a-straddle, into the ditch. Coming up: a barbed wire fence. Fortunately, the ground slams up to meet me before I hit the prongs.

The bike's wrapped around my limbs, and pain — a giant red peony in mind's eye — explodes from my womanly parts, which I've slammed against the crossbar.

T, sole witness, leaps off his bike and is beside me. "Are you okay?"

The pain is blinding. If I could see his eyes, I know I'd view real concern. I can't move. Can't speak. I am slowly becoming aware that I've shaved a fillet of skin off my shin, and my ankle's twisted at an inconceivable angle.

"Ugh."

"Shelley, are you okay? Talk to me."

I make another noise, still don't move. I could easily cry; it hurts so badly, and I don't know if this mess of metal I'm entangled in will even be rideable now. Hell, I may never *stand* again, let alone pedal a bike. Then, I see myself through my estranged husband's eyes. This stupid helmet, my green-clad body semi-buried in grass, eyes a few inches from the wire. And I start to laugh. And he laughs. We laugh and laugh until I'm back on that blessed, indestructible beast, wincing and wobbly — throbbing, too — but on the road again.

"Good thing," I sputter, "that I'm not having sex anymore," which is not entirely true, and he knows it, but it seems the right thing to say.

We meet the kids at the predetermined corner. It's raining rats and mongooses now (another Jesus story), and there are at least three rainbows. We are muck-splattered in our handsome blues and greens. Legs, asses, backs. Even our faces are awash in watery mud.

God, we look great.

We cycle together into artsy Makawao. "The Mexican restaurant's closed," I whine, so looking forward, was I, to a margarita.

"They might have told us," Logan, also thirsty, commiserates.

T suggests we cycle down the main drag.

We eat at a health food-type restaurant with a spotless bathroom. Logan and I order chicken salad: the sandwiches are easily two inches thick. T and Taylor eat slightly slimmer quiche.

Suddenly it's all happening too fast. We're on the backstretch, and it's still early morning. The sky has become another wash of blue and the sun remembers where she needs to be. I want to slow everything down. No, I want to altogether stop time. I want to forever be this family of four momentarily ecstatic adults in maybe-Gore-Tex rain/wind suits, Darth Vader helmets, and mud-splashed, shit-eating grins, fluently soaring down the face of a Hawaiian volcano, even if it is only pretend.

ONCE UPON A TIME IN BALI

His name is Mogly, he's a tailor with a thousand-watt smile, and he's fitting my son for a three-piece suit. I'm not a shopper. I stand outside, dissolving in the nearly equatorial heat. I pluck at my sweat-soaked blouse. A barefoot motorcyclist speeds past with two passengers — a woman and a baby. Yesterday I saw five people on one bike. I'm having some trouble believing my eyes.

"*Ibu*," Logan says, using the Bahasa Indonesian word for *mother*. "I've decided to get *two* suits, and a belt."

Logan and I are unlikely travel-mates. He's twenty-four, and I am not. He lives in Saskatoon and enjoys the urban pace and nightlife. I live in a village of 300 and appreciate hearing coyotes in the evening. I'm all about solitary walks through the campground at dusk, when the light appears blue. Logan earns a respectable income welding farm equipment. I'm a literary writer, and this year will earn less than $10,000. We are mother and son, and we don't see each other often. It might be fair to say that since he's grown up and I've moved away, we no longer know each other well. Now here we are on a street in Kuta, Bali, midway through our ten-day vacation. He is having suits made. I have purchased a fridge magnet. *Bali*, it reads, beneath a grotesque mask. I don't need much more.

When Logan and I began discussing a mother-son vacation, we agreed that our destination must be exotic, inexpensive (for me), and offer good surfing (for him, although I was game, too). Bali seemed to fit the bill, and we booked something called the "Bali Bliss Package," which included our flight from Vancouver, a three-star beach hotel (breakfasts included), five sightseeing tours, and a massage at a high-end spa.

"I won't be using that," Logan said.

After almost fourteen hours of air travel and a hot dog in Taiwan, we arrived in Denpasar. I've travelled in Mexico, the Caribbean, and South America, and I've witnessed wild traffic, but I'd never experienced anything like the motorcycle vs. car-weaving-pinball machine chaos of Balinese streets.

"Well, we won't be renting a motorcycle," I said, as the airport shuttle ripped past yet another Hindu shrine. "That's for damn sure."

Our destination was Sanur, a quieter area than party-central Kuta.

"*Selamat siang*. Good day," I said to the desk clerk at the Inna Sindhu Beach hotel. I was perhaps a bit too proud of the fact that I'd learned some simple Bahasa Indonesian vocab and phrases back in Saskatchewan. I had taught the numbers to ten and simple greetings to Logan while we downed pints in a Jasper pub during our VIA train stop — Saskatoon to our departure city, Vancouver.

"They call this a three-star?" Logan was taking in the blue pools and fountains, the manicured grounds, the carved wood and marble at our "cottage" with the oh-so-welcome air conditioning. "It's awesome!" I agreed. From the super-friendly service to the anything-you-desired breakfasts, from the live music to the oceanside setting, this was a five-star deal.

The beachfront boasted coral reef-sheltered waters, colourful outrigger canoes, and fishermen beneath broad rice hats. They were waist-deep in water.

"I give you massage?" A woman swept her hand across the low tables set in the sand. "*Tidak mau*," I answered. "No thanks."

The boardwalk restaurants appeared endless. We ascertained that a quick way to measure costs was to price compare the popular Indonesian fried rice dish *nasi goreng* at each. We rarely spent over $10 CDN on a meal.

"Cheers, *ibu*," Logan said, hoisting a Bintang, the local beer, on our first night.

"To Bali, *anak laki laki*," I said, clinking bottles. "And to us."

We spent most of our time in Bali on motorcycle.

One moment we were walking past a hand-written *Rentals* sign, and the next Logan was shaking on a deal: "So it's been a while … how do you drive one of these?"

We hired "Dennis" to double me and lead us out of sprawling Denpasar and into Ubud, the centre of Bali's arts scene. I laughed at our helmet-heads, murmured a prayer, and tried to visualize where I'd filed the travel insurance. On the road, I kept turning to ensure that Logan was still behind us; I hadn't seen him grinning that broadly since forever.

Ubud's only about thirty kilometres from Sanur, but it took an hour to arrive at its maze of boutiques, cafés, galleries, and temples. Dennis left us at the central market among a hundred other parked motorcycles.

"Memorize that licence plate number, Logan."

It was a shopping kind of morning. My son had reverse-packed — "I buy as I need it" — and from underwear to blow darts, the market had it all. No change rooms? No problem. Logan joked with the amiable saleswomen as he slipped out of and into shorts. (Months later, I'd still hear the women's melodic "Best price... morning price... only for you." After a sale, they brushed the bills across their merchandise for good luck. I bought three knock-off batiks, mostly so I could barter in their language.)

Perhaps the apple doesn't fall far from the tree; my son and I *do* share a genuine interest in people. I can't include all the friends we made in Bali, but I can tell you about Gede, the twenty-one-year-old who led us into the mountains on motorbike.

"You do realize that if we wipe out, we're dead," I warned Logan as we dodged possibly rabid dogs and side-swiping cars.

"*Ibu, tidak apa apa.*" (Translation: *Ma, don't worry.*)

I didn't... much... and holy *National Geographic*, what a journey. Women balancing baskets on their heads, old men working in the terraced rice fields...

"See that?" Gede pointed, and I glimpsed a smoking pyre. "That's a cremation."

The wind raked my hair as we flew up the road, and it was one surreal moment after the next.

When we reached majestic Mount Batur, Gede asked if we wanted to pay homage to Sariswati (goddess of knowledge) at a nearby temple. "But we must cover ourselves," he said. I pulled out the pseudo batiks, and voilà: sarongs.

No one looked askance at the sole tourists in the bustling *pura*. I sat on the ground and tried to absorb the gamelan music, the priests flicking holy water over worshippers' heads, the high-piled food, flower and incense offerings, the speaker-broadcast prayers.

"I don't believe this," I whispered to Logan. "Do you have any idea how lucky we are?"

Yes, he said, he absolutely did.

We surf and kayak. We eat and drink in live-music bars. We take the public boat across the choppy Bedung Strait to Nusa Lembongan, where we split rooming costs with a Dane and go snorkelling, and Logan stumbles onto a traditional cock fight (the bloody details of which I'll not go into).

The motorcycle offers freedom. We happen onto the Sacred Monkey Forest Sanctuary, where 300 Balinese macaques wander, scrap, scream, and get into decidedly human-like monkey business. We see a Kecak dance. We watch pieceworkers transform silver into works-of-art jewellery. We splash through the streets in water up to our shins. And — ha! — we *both* enjoy that spa massage.

But the highlight's yet to come.

"I want to invite you to my home," Mogly says, surprising us. We've been seeing him every few days, and have already spent an entire afternoon laughing, eating, and singing "American Pie." He's taken us to the textile shop he patronizes, and while Logan selected several metres for his sister in Saskatoon, I swam through the Pasar Badung market's spice and fruit vendors. "Nice skin," the women said, grabbing and stroking my arms.

"Are you sure?" I ask. "We could take you and your family out."

No, he wants to invite us.

The next day we meet at Mogly's shop and follow our friend to the seaside market to buy fish. We follow him through mud-clogged alleys, and past the river that flooded two nights before and reached right to his doorstep. At his modest home, we meet his wife, Sri, and their toddler, and Sri's sister, who lives with them.

Mogly throws coconut shells on the ground, douses them in kerosene, strikes a match, and covers the flames with tin flashing. The fish go on top. Inside, Sri's preparing rice.

We eat on the floor. The food's wonderful, but the fellowship's sublime. We discuss work, customs, language, family, and religion. Mogly, a Muslim on this predominantly Hindu island, addresses the often negative global perception of Muslims. "Extremists form such a tiny percent. Most of us desire peace."

He says the *Shahadah* — *La ilaha ill'Allah, Muhammad rasul Allah* — and reads from the Qur'an. He says he can't go to the mosque tomorrow, because he's had a beer and thus is unclean. He invites us to return, and "next time" to join him in his homeland, Java.

Later I'll lie on my bed in the cottage and say to Logan, in his bed across the room: "We are so alive."

To travel is to learn, and I hope to be a lifelong student. In Bali I learned more through being welcomed into the homes and hearts of the people than I could ever glean from a book. Perhaps from a *dozen* books. I learned that my son travels like a veteran, and that we're excellent travelling companions. And I learned — through watching him interact so delightfully and easily with others — that my kid who is all grown up is going to be okay in life. I could go back to my quiet little village, and it'd be fine if we didn't talk every week or see each other every month.

Once upon a time, we shared the wonders of Bali. And we were so alive.

IN THE FIELD

I STARE OUT THE WINDOW AND — AS A WRITER WITH A poetic persuasion — try to come up with a unique metaphor for the swath. We're into the wheat now. We began with peas; canola, barley, and oats remain. Am I really here, operating this Case International 1666 combine? Are these my hands controlling the speed and the header? I don't quite believe this.

My first time out, after a test run with Michell Heidecker, who with her husband Lyal runs Triple H Farm, near Middle Lake, Saskatchewan, I wasn't sure if I was in a dream or a painting. Dust and tree cotton floated across my vision, hawks were continually lifting off the bristled land, and in the distance, the smooth blue surface of Middle Lake — the actual lake, not the village in which I've lived for the last two years — offered both textural and colour contrast to the acres of swathed fields.

There's no doubt about it: this land is sexy. Slightly rolling, with painterly trees delineating fields, and occasional woodland areas that appeal to the nature-loving explorer in me. But as a novice on this machine, I don't spend too much time daydreaming. The truth: I could use more than a single pair of eyes for this job.

I have one eye on the power monitor, another on the pins that show how much height the header has. I watch for rocks. I keep check on the chaff in my rearview mirror and intermittently observe the grain as it fills the hopper, ensuring that the separator is doing its job, and that the hopper's not going to overflow. I try not to overcorrect my steering and thus leave a wavy line for Taryn, fifteen, who will bale the straw later. I watch for the other combine — almost a twin to this one, with its Saskatchewan flag waving back at my Canadian counterpart.

I listen to how the whole thing works, and if I hear the machinery protest — a sound not unlike the low warning growl of a large dog — I slow down. Sometimes I have to inch through a swath. Sometimes my speed can hit 2.8, or 3, where the swaths are particularly thin. I learn how to use the reverse gear to regurgitate potentially choking chunks. "Rats' nests," Michell calls them.

I remain alert, but after a few rounds I feel my body relax a tad. I turn on the radio: CBC is good for several rounds, then I tune in to the Melfort station. I'm serenaded by the Eagles, Gordon Lightfoot, and other 1970s soft-rock artists. It's absolutely perfect.

Occasionally, not having too much time to make a decision is a good thing. When Lyal asked if I wanted to help with harvest, I decided within seconds that yes, although it was entirely new to me, I very much did. Given days or even minutes to consider, I'm certain I would have chickened out. And I did have experience, of a sort. I once worked in an echinacea field. A little lifetime ago, I spent three years behind the till at the Saskatoon Co-op Farm Centre. I've long been a gardener. Did it count that my sister married a farmer? I added up my paltry inventory; it wasn't much, but hopefully I'd prove a quick study.

I have myriad questions, and when Michell or Lyal flank me with the grain truck — auger out, open hopper — there are a few moments to ask them. What class of wheat is this? (Hard red spring) What do you hope it tests at? (14) How long does harvest take, on average? (Up to six weeks) Least favourite task? (Dealing with breakdowns, and thawing water bowls when it's -40).

I adore the jargon. "We're going to peel this crop off next," Lyal says. Even the words themselves — *feeder, auger, separator, hopper, rotor* — possess an aurally pleasant heft.

Lyal checks the sieves and adjusts the rotor. "There, go make some dust," he says. And I do. But after several hours, the feeder chooses not to run. It rolls for a few seconds, then stops. It's teasing me. I don't want to call for help, though there's a cell phone and the Heideckers' instructions: *If you have any concerns, call.* I try the feeder again. Same thing. I let it rest, try again. At last. It's only been five minutes, but I quickly learn that time has a different value during harvest. A five-minute delay feels more like thirty.

Everything runs along smoothly until after the hopper's emptied again. There's no way the feeder wants to cooperate this time, so I call. "It did this a few years ago," Lyal says, and quads back to his shop. He returns with what looks like — and perhaps is — an extended coat hanger. While he's addressing the problem, the phone rings and the other driver, Kevin — Lyal's cousin from Vancouver — says his header has a flat tire. Lyal shows me where to plug in a wire if the feeder proves stubborn again, then he's off.

By my third field I feel some degree of confidence, but I'm miles from being even half as adept as Michell. Born and raised in Vancouver, she works side by side with Lyal, and to see that mother of four — and manager of an immense garden — take a flawless curve on the combine, or empty the grain truck, or even test grain, is a wonder to my apprenticing eyes.

And there's something else I'm witnessing: how the children pitch in, and don't complain, and make it all seem joyful. Today they're in the potato field; there'll be a potato pancake feast tonight. The kids make meals and tend the chickens. They weed and pick vegetables and care for their 4-H steers. How different their lives from that of my (now grown) offspring.

I'm a writer who takes on other employment because I can't afford not to. I'm a woman beginning to love the way the combine's shadow chases it, and how when I turn a corner, the light changes so significantly it's like a brand new day. I love how peas shooting into the hopper sound like high-powered popcorn. I love cucumber sandwiches and homemade cookies delivered to the field in a brown paper bag. I love the hum of it all, and the heat on my arms and back.

I don't have a metaphor for the swaths. You know they are golden. You know how the light catches the kernels and makes them dazzle. The swaths are what they are. They are swaths, and that is enough. Harvest is a kind of poetry.

PLENTY OF FISH

Lukas, a Swiss lover I once enjoyed at a multi-disciplinary artists' retreat, e-mails me the treatment for a documentary on the New Orleans jazz pioneer Johnny St. Cyr. The film will be in English, and Lukas wants me to cast an editorial eye over his synopsis. "Just fix the wirst mistakes," he writes, but I don't, I fix them all.

It is -30° C, too cold to run for my usual hour today. Not enough sweaters, coats, socks or scarves to buffer the prairie wind. What will I miss? A few days ago, two healthy coyotes eyed me from a field and I gave it right back to them. Then a white creature, low to the ground and slinking, black-tipped tail. Ermine. Or short-tailed weasel (but I prefer *ermine*).

The woods are mostly full of surprises, and within them I feel best.

But today I will not run. I turn my attention to Lukas's treatment.

> Banjoist and guitarist Johnny St. Cyr performed with scores
> of big name musicians throughout the 1920s, including
> Joe "King" Oliver. He was integral to Louis Armstrong's
> Hot Five (1925-1928) and Hot Seven (1927) recording
> sessions at Okeh studios; headlined Johnny St. Cyr's Young
> Men from New Orleans late in life; and was recognized as a
> founding father of jazz banjo and guitar, yet little has been
> documented about this enigmatic musician.

Exile is a lonely country. I hadn't anticipated the severe melancholia that would grip me in my adopted Saskatchewan village of 300 goodly — and mostly Germanic — souls. I had been desperate to get away from the city and start my life over, and now I was yearning for the friends, family, home, and long-time husband I'd walked away from.

I've tried. I've made huge vegetable gardens and shared the harvests. I've five-pin bowled with the seniors and drunk bitter coffee from Styrofoam cups with the farmers in the post office/liquor outlet/Sears catalogue depot. I've written poems in a Mexican hammock strung between the gate post I helped set in concrete and a giant, cone-spitting spruce. I've tracked the hummingbirds in my delphiniums and listened to the not-so-distant buzz of speedboats and jet-skis. I've frequented abandoned railroad tracks and counted garter snakes (fifty-two is the one-hike record), run down country roads past skunks, badgers, Arabian horses and coyotes. I've spent time face down in a clearing in the woods. Holiest of holies: a doe leapt over my shoulder. I've hiked through the poplar, aspens and saskatoons to Lucien Lake, nine minutes from my door, and circled the woodland campground until I've become familiar with all the nests, the berries, and where to find heaps of hazelnuts. Snow geese rise off the water in a confederation of wings. I've picked ticks off my neck and legs (twenty-two is the one-day record). On Sundays I've attended the Lutheran Church at the end of my sidewalk and sat alone in the third pew from the back, left side. The good villagers have given me crocheted dishcloths, fresh fish, zucchini. I've become thin. My eyes and teeth too big for my face. I have not seen my children much.

I am a mess. A puddle. I make videos of myself sobbing and trying to reconcile the disaster that is my life. "Melancholia 1." "Melancholia 2." I eat meals alone. Watch the sun set alone. Play the piano for no one. I wake during the depths of night and step outside to consider the universe, the stars so close I feel I could pick them off the sky. I am alone. I am running ten kilometres as fast as I can almost every single day, but I've also completely lost the will to breathe.

Desperate times and measures. I meet Carl on www. plentyoffish.com. The velocity of his attraction to me is terrifying: a mini lifetime, fast-tracked. We meet (virtually); communicate (a few e-mails); he professes love, then, when I ease back, despair. He verbally abuses me, we "split." After step three, *love*, he'd suggested a rendezvous "in a few days," and I explained why that would be impossible: I live in another province. Apparently in my various responses to prospective "Long-term" hopefuls, I failed to include this detail to Carl in my earliest messages.

He writes: "I get about 1 in 20 replies to my emails on POF. Maybe 1 in 10 of those wants to meet for coffee. About half of those don't show up or call. 75% of the ones that do have so much baggage or lies or some unbelievable bullshit I have almost lost faith there are any decent women left in Canada. I only want one 'hit'. Someone having the same interests comes in at about 1 in a 1000 emails. I have been on and off POF 3 years now and have had 8 dates: 3 remain friends. Of one of the 8, I was her 3rd date of 4 in one day, 2 spent the entire date telling me of the horrendous abuse they endured from men whose cultures have honour killings, and the other 2 checked out every guy within 50 paces to the point of having a neck injury.

"Great, now you! We don't need to import BS from out of province here! Why don't you delete your profile and start again? I won't view you and if you don't view me it won't show on the list. I think it's the decent thing to do but, at this point I wonder if you have that in you. Don't write me as this is the last communication."

Jesus, we're a sad and lonely lot.

A day passes. It's colder than Mars, so of course I go outside to put up my Christmas lights. A single string of white mini-lights, wrangled around my gate. My neighbour's house and fence are ablaze. Blinking reindeer prance across her snow-sheathed lawn. I feel like putting up a sign with an arrow: "Ditto."

Carl writes again: "I was very excited about the possibility to get to know you. Quite a bit more than I have been with anyone since I signed up with online dating. I have recently conjured a way to automate the manufacture of artificial limestone for bas relief, flat or curved panels for corporate lobbies and boardrooms. I am taking some marketing classes next week. Conservative estimates on this procedure with some low tech equipment and 4 labourers show it to have an unbelievable potential. I can make 300 sq. ft @$75 per ft so that's approx. $20,000 per day net before taxes. I can manufacture this anywhere. After a year or maybe 2 I plan on franchising and making much finer and more elaborate accessory items. I have been working on a line of very fine wall sconces taken from classic urn and vase shapes. These will be cast in Scagliola to emulate semi-precious stone such as turquoise and lapis lazuli. This also can be done anywhere and in addition to my other neoclassic items can be sold online.

"I'll bet there are very few men in Calgary, Winnipeg, Toronto, or any other cities you do searches in that have the potential (or will) to accompany you in your rural lifestyle and desire to travel. Those are exactly the things I want. And I want to build an almost completely self-sufficient home decorated with mosaics and eco art. I would have no problem living almost anywhere in Canada (as long as we travelled south in the winter), and I love the woods, canoeing and the flora and fauna of your area.

"I am a dedicated, caring, unbelievably romantic lover and would not have hesitated to mesh with your lifestyle and to encourage and nurture your art and dreams. But here we are now. Carl."

The message was sent from a BlackBerry device on the Rogers Wireless Network.

I try to resist the temptation to respond to Carl. Don't possess that degree of willpower. I write:

We wouldn't be human if we didn't make mistakes from time to time, and I appreciated your apology, but I found your previous messages, well … unusually cruel … and disturbing. I was shocked. I'm not used being spoken to in that way, and I'm not the class of woman who tolerates it.

I understand your frustration. Here we are, living in a world where communication is quicker, easier and cheaper (if not free) than ever before, and yet the world is full of aching men and women who want nothing more than to connect with someone else, yet we're unable to. So it's a sadness, indeed.

It would be best if we said farewell at this point. I hope you find someone incredibly interesting and absolutely perfect for you, Carl. I wish you the very best, personally and professionally.

(And perhaps it is a surprise, but it appears that almost everyone who has contacted me desires the *Harrowsmith* lifestyle, even if it *is* Saskatchewan-style.)

Farewell, brief friend.

There was another candidate, from Coeur d'Alene, Idaho. A woodcarver and high-end furniture maker. He used five-syllable words and competed in triathlons; I was hopeful. Then came the kicker: he told me he had not "coupled" with a woman for thirty years.

And there have been those who've made me laugh. The guy who wrote: "Shite, now I know why I haven't been receiving any hits on my profile...I accidently typed that I'm less than five feet tall."

Carl sends another message. "I get games played on me on almost a daily basis on POF, and am tired of lies, deception, and outright cruelty. I should have just deleted your message at first. I find it exceedingly rude and gluttonous the number of women that will read and not reply to messages. Take this as you will. I am sorry I am angry at not being able to find an honest, truthful woman online. There is a 6 to 1 ratio on POF and the horror stories I hear about the 'popular' men would make you delete your profile. If you stay on I think you would do well to be a little more forthcoming. Farewell."

This is also sent from a BlackBerry device on the Rogers Wireless Network.

I block Carl.

I wrap in layers: double everything, including the scarves, and walk to the post office for my mail. A friend has sent a package that smells like good Italian soap. It is enough to sail me through. Then a walk in the woods. Only animals have been in the park: deer and coyote, raccoon and rabbit. And magpies big as toasters. Often I stop to hear the trees moan against each other.

In the deeper woods, where I never see human prints, it is tempting to lie in a shaft of light like a child about to make a snow angel. Sometimes I do. Sometimes I do.

At home the almost-finished bottle of merlot sits on the counter where I left it last night. A new friend came over, and shared her various grievances with me. People have always opened to me in this way. I am a listener.

E-mails. There are January specials to the Algarve. Someone has changed her e-address. Membership fees are due.

I phone a neighbour I don't know well, inviting him and his wife to my Christmas potluck. He takes this invitation like one who's been invited to step up to a guillotine. Not a word of appreciation or an atom of enthusiasm. "Well, thank you!" I say. "Let me know!"

I run a bath, and realize with fresh clarity that I may well grow old alone. I did not expect to. The thing is, I like my men to be brilliant. Lukas is. He knows the difference between *wirst* and *worst*. And he knows I know he knows.

In the bath, for a few moments, it seems like growing old alone might be okay. Maybe. Mostly I want to shred my own skin because I so do *not* want to be alone, not even for one night.

Lukas. Long married to a fabric artist. We were happy. How desperate — I mean beyond even Plenty-of-Fish desperate — I am in jeopardy of becoming. Take this, for example: I was in the city not long ago, and I swear the busker sitting on a scrap of cardboard outside the liquor store, strumming and singing his heart out — he had a decent voice — gave me pause, and if the coin had landed the other way, I would have invited him to spend the rest of his life with me.

My front room walls are like cream and within them it is as quiet as a tomb. I read in the sunlight. I finish off the last half of the tin of chocolate icing I purchased yesterday for a cake I may *need* to make. Spoon to mouth. Spoon to mouth. It doesn't matter.

Last night I finally brought out the Christmas tree the previous owners had left, dismantled, in the crawlspace. I don't give a whit about Christmas trees, or Christmas, but just in case my adult kids and their partners *do* visit over the holidays — I'm such a downer, even *I* wouldn't visit me — I want to make an effort. I set the tree up: there are eight-inch gaps between branches, and it leans. I decorate: lights first (three strings), then the decorations, which go back to my earliest days as a wife, as a mother, as all those earlier incarnations, and I realize why I haven't put up a tree for years. But there it is, weighted with gold pears and sugared apples; with opulent balls and hand-stitched stockings; with bells and bows and — only because I am feeling generous — a solitary Santa. House lights off, tree lights up. Then the tree's plastic base cracks from the weight. Major crash and impressive shattering. A comedy of errors. And I don't care.

I pluck off the strings of beads and sweep up the glass, pitch the tree into the backyard. Dump day is Saturday.

They say there's always something when you're a homeowner. Yes. Pipes drip, and the chain on my garage door recently snapped and almost took me out. There is always something. Today I can't open my door. The lock refuses the key. Could the busker have dealt with this?

St. Cyr was born April 17th, 1890 in New Orleans, and by fifteen was already a self-taught musician. One can speculate that growing up in multi-ethnic and multi-racial New Orleans at the turn of the century—with its melting pot of musical styles, ranging from spirituals and folks songs to brass marching bands and opera—was metaphorically rich. African drums and dance were the heartbeat of New Orleans' Congo Square. In Storyville (where musicians provided the veritable soundtrack for prostitution and gambling until the US Navy shut down the red light district in 1917, as sailors were suffering from the district's flourishing crime and venereal disease); in the dance halls; in the small, smoky speakeasies; and on the Mississippi riverboats that crawled across the muddy waters, St. Cyr and his contemporaries were musically engaged at every corner. It is not surprising that jazz—or "jass," as it was first called, perhaps in reference to orgasm—began in this exhilarating environment.

New Orleans was an intersection where grinding poverty, the experience of downtrodden African Americans, the swamps' damp heat, fancy society picnics at Lake Pontchartrain, funeral processions, Voodoo and Hoodoo religions, and the music of various languages (including French and Spanish) merged and culminated in the unique sounds that spread north to Chicago, New York, and beyond, and have influenced music to the present day.

The friend who visited last night unspooled a tale of woe, and during it I fantasized about her brother (twice married, with school-aged children and an alcoholic wife), and how much I hope his marriage fails and he thinks of me and gets up the nerve to call when his wife's in rehab, and later, while they're going through the divorce, our hands will meet above or below a table and we'll be happy with our bandaged families in our wake, and maybe there's a reason I live alone in a village without even a dog to hug. Patience is the least of my meagre virtues.

POF: message from a displaced New Brunswicker. Jean Roy. Art history degree. Elementary school teacher. Fantastic on-line repartee. I haul out my grade eleven French notes. *Ça va?* The flurry of messages begins. One wonders how anyone can be that good-looking and find themselves in the murky, desolate, ridiculous, spirit-shattering sewer that is free online dating.

A cornucopia of major artists helped shape jazz across the decades—exceptionally talented men and women with tragic and/or scintillating personal lives and technicolourful careers. Johnny (Buddy) St. Cyr did not possess the braggadocio of Jelly Roll Morton or the charisma of Louis Armstrong; did not experience a caravan fire and have his fingers welded together like Django Reinhardt; did not invent hip jargon like Lester Young; did not influence fashion like Dizzy Gillespie; did not humble his contemporaries like blind Art Tatum; innovate like Duke Ellington; or drink himself to death like Bix Beiderbecke. St. Cyr stayed drug-free and out of jail and asylums. Here is a man who made jazz history *without* succumbing to vice.

I somehow manage to lose a pork roast and a package of lean ground beef between the grocery store and home. I usually exist on homemade soup and homemade bread. I never thought I would be the kind of person who cooked. Or baked. My husband-of-decades was the cook. What I did *not* lose was the 450-gram tin of Duncan Hines Creamy Home-Style Chocolate frosting — all gone now. Nutrition Facts: Per 2 tablespoons of chocolate frosting (35g): Calories/140; Fat Saturated + Trans)/9%; Cholesterol/0mg; Sodium/4%; Carbohydates/7% (Fibre /4%; Sugars 0); Protein/0; Vitamin A, C + Calcium/0; Iron/4%.

Hurray for the iron.

POF: Felipe. "(i am a latino from south america looking for fun and friendship with the right girl. i am funny and very friendly person also not into head games because we dont have time for that do we? the woman i want is emotionally connected with me before we make love or do anything naughty! i am strong and fit also, into sports and excercize. if you like to hang out with a cool, confident guy from down south contact me for a nice time together)."

I say hello, in the POF way. He writes: "te propongo algo … dame una chase de ablar de ablar espanol con tigo un poquieto, no me rechases. los dos nos pedemos befeficiar de unas bueans comberscaiones. ok camon dont be so hard ……"

Who could not be entertained by this? Spelling mistakes in his own language. These are the types of *comberscaiones* I often have.

There are good things I could do. I have twice practised my repertoire of Christmas carols on the piano: I could play for the seniors at the nursing home beside the lake. Many of them are suffering from dementia and can no longer speak; the perfect audience for one who rarely plays. I could pick up the phone and wish everyone who matters to me a merry Christmas. It's in the giving, as they say. But even that can be wrenching: Valentine's Day, 2008: I sent fourteen valentines and did not receive a single one back.

Grief is a dress I don't want in my closet any more. (Melancholy is more palatable when simultaneously melodramatic.)

I prepare for a date. I am meeting Donald at a lounge in the city. It takes an incredible amount of nerve for me to speak to him on the phone. At first I dislike his voice — higher than I'd hoped — but then I start to think of it as sexy. Again: raging hopes. I adore his photos. He's dark, and wears a hat, and when I look at his images I think: this one beats to a different drum.

I buy new panties. They are not sexy, but they are black. I have my son's girlfriend drive me to said lounge. I am a few minutes early; Donald is not there. Thank God. I am desperate to commence with the drinking — I feel like I'm about to be interviewed for a job (and/or I'm thirteen, and the principal at Jonas Samson Junior High has called me to the office for pulling boys into the girls' washroom) — but know that wouldn't look good.

I watch the stairs while trying not to watch the stairs. And there he is, a shrunken version of the man I viewed online; if he's six feet tall, I'm Gwyneth Paltrow. I guess that his posted photos are at least a decade old. In the interim, he seems to have lost some of the important teeth.

And he tries so hard it breaks my heart.

After an hour and a half, I excuse myself, and flee to the bathroom. I have my cell phone, and dial my son's girlfriend: *Twenty minutes, please. Rescue me at the A&W next door.*

I am forty-six years old. Dating does not become me, but solitude (and life *sans* sex) is a far less attractive option.

> Wikipedia: Johnny St. Cyr (April 17, 1890 in New Orleans, Louisiana–June 17, 1966 in Los Angeles, California) was an American jazz banjoist and guitarist. He is most commonly remembered as a member of Louis Armstrong's Hot Five and Hot Seven bands, as well as the early ensemble recordings led by Jelly Roll Morton. From 1961 until his death in 1966, St. Cyr was the bandleader of the Young Men From New Orleans, who performed at Disneyland.

Lukas writes: "What a poor English I have. It must be funny reading my letters. Thank God you have experience with kid's writing."

He responds to my comment about the cold weather. He says a friend — a former principal ballerina with La Scala Opera Company — is currently in Siberia, and it is cold there, too.

My POF profile:
A few things I like (off the top of my head):

1. September... for the climate, the colours, the back-to-it-ness

2. Latin music/culture and speaking Spanish

3. passionate kissing

4. discussing films (as opposed to movies)

5. playing piano and guitar by ear

6. the woods (very much; I live across from them, and explore them every day)

7. multi-generational friendships

8. how horses don't know they are beautiful

9. growing my own food, and filling my rooms with flowers from my garden

10. Louise Malle's *Damage*, Altman's *Short Cuts*, and, of course, brilliant Canadian films like *My Life Without Me* and *Away From Her*

11 meeting interesting people in unexpected places

12. sheets dried on the clothesline

13. politeness and good grammar

14. CBC radio (usually)

15. books, films, music, paintings, etc. that make me think and feel. And good photographs. I love good photographs

16. galleries (the National Gallery in London... the Rodin Museum in Paris... and tiny, unassuming galleries featuring the work of local, contemporary artists)

17. reconnecting with friends I went to school with and learning that we can still be the girls/boys we were back then

18. a hearty laugh

19. artist retreats (new landscapes and interiors never fail to inspire me)

20. the work of many American writers, including T.C. Boyle, Raymond Carver, Ann Beattie, Robert Boswell, Antonya Nelson, Annie Dillard, etc. (though I tend to read Canadian first)

21. men at least 6 feet tall (especially if they can dance)

Dislikes

1. rednecks and obnoxious drunks

2. generic POF biographies, plus "I seen" and "alot," and the use of the word "Lady" on online dating sites

3. loud cars and/or trucks, and booming bass

4. my own ignorance about many things ... world history ... art ... politics ... architecture ... changing tires

5. Facebook (though I've succumbed)

6. superlatives, i.e.: when someone says something like: He's the nicest person you could ever meet

7. generalizations, i.e.: Every little girl dreams of her [traditional] wedding

8. that so few Canadians read CanLit

9. shopping (not into fashion—I'm a blue jeans and white blouse or black turtleneck type)

10. cooking

11. Achilles tendonitis

12. weeds, or, rather, not having time to deal with them

13. football, or any televised sport (prefer to *play* sports, not watch them)

14. materialism, fundamentalism, homophobia, racism, sexism

15. television (but own one to watch the news)

16. sleeping alone

17. ATVs and Sea-Doos (please don't respond if this is what you're into)

18. the price of good running shoes

19. not having enough hours in the day, ever

20. small dogs (but I adore large dogs)

21. cell phones (I've never texted anyone in my life)

I fall into something online. He lives in Dawson City. He flies to Saskatoon on a business trip. We meet, and he is ideal, and I kiss him three times. We have one hour together, then he flies home, and I drive back to my village. I have no idea what he thinks of me. I want this so badly I would move to Dawson City tomorrow. How much is too much e-mailing? Mostly I watch my computer screen. I even pray a little: *God, You know better than anyone how much I need this.* Oh, please.

Many early New Orleans musicians, particularly African Americans like St. Cyr and other guitar-based blues players, were self-taught improvisers who could not read music, or anything else. The classically trained Creole musicians with whom they often played — especially after the so-called Black Code of 1894 enforced a ruling that anyone of African descent would henceforth be considered black and could not work with whites — resulted in Downtown Creoles and Uptown blacks working together more, though some Creoles maligned the blacks' "ratty" music.

Besides guitar and banjo, St. Cyr also played a self-invented six-string guitar-banjo: a guitar neck attached to a banjo pot. [Lukas: could you work this in somewhere else? It's out of place here.] His leap into a full-time musical career came when he received the opportunity to work on the famous Mississippi riverboats with pianist and band leader Fate Marble in 1917.

St. Cyr's last summer on the boats was 1921; he played with the Creath band. In the fall he left the band

and the boats for good and returned to New Orleans. Later, in Chicago, St. Cyr hooked up with King Oliver's Creole Jazz Band, and with Jelly Roll Morton and his Red Hot Peppers. His greatest fame, however, came with Louis Armstrong's Hot Five and Hot Seven recordings.

Around 1930, St. Cyr returned to New Orleans, where he played regularly as an itinerant musician and continued to supplement his income by working as a plasterer. In 1955 the sixty-five-year-old packed up his banjo and left his hometown forever. He became a regular performer at Disneyland (1961-1966). He called his band in Disneyland—land of Mickey Mouse and Peter Pan—The Young Men from New Orleans. Walt Disney was apparently a huge fan, and "New Orleans Square" was officially opened and dedicated on July 24, 1966.

Jean Roy is the saddest man I've ever met. His life's gone completely off the rails. How could I have gleaned this from those witty, intellectual e-mails? When I meet him in the flesh, I see that he is fifty pounds heavier (at least) than his online photos. He has nicotine stains on his fingers. He shares dead dog and dead mother and my-partner-left-me stories. He is carless, jobless, and does not have enough money to pay for his own beer. He'd checked himself into a hospital recently because he just couldn't take it. A woman destroyed him. *Love* destroyed him. This is Love's other job.

I am the last person who should be giving any kind of advice, but I find myself using platitudes like "Keep the faith. Good things will be ahead for you." And I believe it, if he can pick up the shards of his life. I think he lives in some kind of flophouse, but he has an appealing smile. Part of me wants to make him a project. Save the Lonely Heart. Who am I kidding? I can't even save myself.

When I tell him online that I won't be seeing him again, "because I'm not emotionally strong enough to be with someone who is also struggling…" he has a far more impressive freak-out than Carl. My favourite bits include: "What did you expect: George Clooney, Brad Pitt, or Tiger Woods? Sorry, but I'm more of a Dustin Hoffman. You will find plenty of guys on this website who adore pounding back beer in front of a television football game or shining their Ford F-150. Sorry, I am more interested in global issues and politics than a Flames game."

I block Jean Roy. I hope he glues his life back together. I really do.

Dawson City is rationing his communication with me. One e-mail per day. And little indication of where his head and heart are at. I'd best face it: he's slipping away. I watch the clock, do the math of hours between time zones. Decide I will wait until 3:00 his time to share my feelings. Then make it 5:00. He is so beautiful. And intelligent. A big tree I want to climb, possibly forever.

I write the make or break e-mail.

Subject line: *Do Still Waters Run Deep?* And I begin with this: "Basho told a disciple that the trouble with most poems was that they were either subjective or objective, and when the disciple said, 'You mean, too subjective or too objective?' Basho said, 'No.'"

I scarcely know you, but already I may be investing too much hope in possibility. Only you know. Or do you?

Forgive me, but I need some clue, however minute. Please select the response that best fits your feelings re: the *potential* for an *us*.

a) The jury's still in deliberation. Will get back to you at my earliest convenience. [aka: the *safe* response. What it really imparts is that there's a greater chance of Christ returning tomorrow and playing "Purple Haze" with Jim Morrison at a free concert in Central Park — with Elvis, Karen Carpenter, JFK, and my maternal grandmother sitting front and centre on a Hudson's Bay blanket — than us hooking up.]

b) Probably not, but thanks for your interest, and now PFO.

c) I like you, but fear you might become bored, thus my reticence.

d) The timing's not right. So solly. It was nice to meet you. (aka: the *gentlemanly* response)

e) You're an unusual woman, and I'm intrigued. Please stand by. I'll let you know within _____ (insert number) of days. (You won't be held to this).

f) Almost yes. (aka: Highly likely)

g) Yes.

(Please note: <u>I'm only enquiring about *potentiality* here, nothing more.</u> It's just a little guide. For me. Because I've never "dated" in my life. But I felt something; I *feel* something. You can answer in pencil.)

St. Cyr continued to perform at Disneyland until his death—from unknown causes—in 1966. From the musical streets of New Orleans to the popular Mississippi riverboats, from hot Chicago clubs to the surreal landscape of Disneyland, Johnny St. Cyr was a jazz great whose brilliance has been obscured by the shadows of the legends he worked with. Clearly, he enjoyed a life well-lived; unfortunately the world does not know enough about it. Someone should make a documentary.

Lukas forgets that when we met he told me that the ballerina is his lover. She lives in Milan, and she is his brother's wife. Yes, he forgets. I remind him. He writes that apparently his lovers prefer cold weather. I believe we will always be friends.

ONE MONTH IN MAZATLÁN

IMPRESIONES Y LAMENTOS

WE HAVE INTERESTING NEIGHBOURS IN MEXICO. A BOA constrictor lounges in the poly-armed tree metres from the back patio, and a *loro*, surely the jolliest bird on earth — or at least the most verbose — melodically greets passersby with a cherubic *hola*, strings of incomprehensible Spanish, and, occasionally, wolf whistles. Just now the bird is holding forth with the tune "The more we get together, the happier we'll be." I freaking love this bird. There are also stray dogs, a medical doctor, the Corresponsalia Consular de Italia, Father Tovar's Home for Boys, a disgraced Mazatleco lawyer, and a sprinkling of expats. One neighbour tells us: "That guy, in the house with elevator —" she points to the adjacent hillside and a contemporary white mansion with multiple levels, "he could be a pedophile, or maybe he's just a pimp."

We're in our final days of this month-long vacation. My partner, G, dreams of spending winters in Mexico once he retires from teaching; in many ways this feels less like a holiday and more like a trial run. G has just hiked down the hill to the embarcadero to catch the 20-peso boat that ferries passengers to the seemingly endless and endlessly seductive Stone Island — Isla de Piedra — where he'll make the most of the sun and waves, and almost certainly enjoy a strawberry margarita, beachside. He'll be approached approximately ninety times by vendors hawking jewellery, "name brand" sunglasses, temporary tattoos, beer holders, and toys, all sorts. No cruise ship hulking in the port today, so the beach will be somewhat less animated.

We bought a boogie board. We're both nudging fifty, but get us out in the water and glory be: children again. G's seen a stingray, and reports hammerheads in the transparent curl of waves. I've been stung by jellyfish; it felt like having my scalp intermittently jabbed by a few hundred well-sharpened knitting needles.

We need reprieves from the heat. Sometimes, with the humidity, it's 48° Celsius. I'm not a "heat" person, but even I have somewhat acclimatized. Today I ran ten kilometres along the concrete *malecón* that hugs the bay-curving beaches, and watched fisherman haul in silver catches. Most impressive: a swordfish one guy jigged right off the shore.

When I run I greet others. Athletes and those giving it a fair shot, giddy children, and the pairs of older women who sway along the *malecón* arm-in-arm, hips moving in a Bessie Smith "St. Louis Blues" kind of way, in unconscious tandem with the waves. Anyone of a certain age uses rags to lethargically flick at sweat and flies.

Presently I am back in the hilltop house we've rented, waiting again for technicians from a cable company to repair the Internet and telephone connections. The system went down five days ago, and every morning I'm promised action. Yesterday I called again on a borrowed phone. I began in English and concluded in rather colourful Spanish, explaining that there were *emergencias con mis hijos* in Canada, and I had to communicate with the darlings *ahorita*.

(There are no real emergencies with my children — adults, both — but they are gypsies, like their mother: one's diving with sharks around the Great Barrier Reef, and the other's moving from Saskatoon to Montreal, maybe today.)

While I wait for the promised visit from the technician, I peruse *NorOeste*, the city's major newspaper. There, on the front page, is exactly what has been calling into question what I thought I believed. Today's headline: "Ejecutan a jefe policiaco en un día de 13 muertes." "Police Chief Killed in a Day of 13 Murders." Also among the dead, the director of Protection Services for the Secretary of Public Security and three of his escorts, who were murdered at 2:50 p.m. in the capital, Culiacán, and two six-year-olds — the daughter and niece of another murdered Mazatleco — who were caught in machine gun crossfire. Every day graphic photographs of those assassinated — shot, machete-hacked, discovered with bags or shirts pulled over their heads, if they indeed still possess a head — are displayed on the front page. The news is saturated with tales of gruesome executions, drug

wars, the dead, the wounded…and descriptions of the
vehicles the perps got away in. Murders are up more than
fifty percent over 2009.

To today's date, August 22, 2010, there have been 247
violent deaths in Mazatlán…an average of 1.06 persons
assassinated per day. June was particularly bad; twenty-eight
of the forty-seven murders took place inside the Centro
de Ejecución de las Consecuencias Jurídicas del Delito
(aka jail). The way bodies have been mounting this month,
August homicides could easily shatter the record.

Today's *NorOeste* reveals that police and the three levels
of government have had enough. "*Tenemos que tomar medidas,*"
says the Subprocurador de Justicia de la zona Sur, Sergio
Avendaño Coronel. *We have to take action.* Octavio Crespo,
Presidente de Ejecutivos de Venta y Mercadotecnia (Sales
and Marketing Management), says authorities are "*contra la
pared.*" *Against the wall.* Of course, merchants are hurting as a
result of this tsunami of violence, as are realtors, restaurateurs,
hoteliers, the shrimp ladies, taxi drivers, dentists…

I no longer buy my own liberal assertion that these
things only happen to those involved with the criminal
element. Among the dozens of assassinations in the few
weeks I've been in this port city, there have been three
murders in public places…the normally innocuous sites
thousands of lawful locals and tourists patronize every day.
Two people were killed on the *malecón* — an eight-year-old
boy was also injured — and another was shot dead outside a
store in an entirely ordinary neighbourhood.

We've had a near-miss, too. G and I escaped being in
the line of machine gun fire by a margin of fifteen minutes

the night we decided to cab home rather than walk our usual route. Our cab was diverted around the crime scene, but not before I witnessed three young men in a police car. I saw eyes. But these were not, as I initially believed, the eyes of an assassin. I read the next day — as I read each day — a description of the vehicle involved and plate numbers, and that once again the police had made no arrests.

~

Sometimes, before one arrives at a destination, one has a notion of what it might look and feel like. I had a preconceived idea — part dream, part research-based, part revelation from a friend proudly born and raised here — about Mazatlán, and surprise of all surprises, I had this city pegged.

Firstly, it is not Puerto Vallarta, which, with its cobblestone streets and well-swept downtown is positively *genteel* in comparison. It is not Mérida, the other Mexican city I've spent a month in. Mérida's a magical *ciudad* with a strong Mayan presence, picturesque squares, and dancing in the streets. I once left my purse on a public bus in Mérida and got it back; these things make an impression.

Mazatlán is gritty. It is falling to its bloodied knees. A delegation from the tourism industry is off to Canada to promote "Maz" as a vacation destination to prospective visitors from Edmonton, Calgary, Vancouver, and Saskatoon. *Buena suerte*, I say. *Good luck*.

But there have also been diamantine moments here, like being invited into the humble home of Julia and her irrepressibly charming thirteen-year-old *hijo* Jorge, who seeks out English conversation in bars. Julia treated us to the *dulces* she bakes on a stove that looks like it has been repeatedly bombed, then pelted with acid rain for a good millennium. She sells her delicious sweets to businesses.

A few days ago, when my friend Juan José was taking us on a trip to the village of Cobala and his fan belt snapped on the highway, he called *his* friend, Arial, who immediately offered his own car and took time off work (at *NorOeste*) to deliver it.

Wow. (Do I have friends I could call to come to the rescue in a similar situation? No way, José.)

And last night, a musician friend of a friend treated us to a salmon meal in his home, shared his poetry and recordings, then played "New York, New York" on a double bass.

But the carnage, the carnage. I'm oversimplifying to beat the band, but it was explained to me that much of the trouble here began in 2007.

"Corn," my friend said, "it's about corn." Sinaloa's a leading corn producer, providing the grain for both Mexican consumption and international export, and when corn prices skyrocketed, "the government essentially doubled production."

Now think tortillas. A staple in Mexico. Tortillas are made with corn. The thing is, corn and marijuana are excellent growing partners — the former also provides a necessary camouflage — so with the increased production of corn, you have increased production of marijuana, which means *narcotraficantes*, cartels, drug wars, and the proliferation of AK-47 "goat horn" assault rifles in the streets.

~

I am only a visitor here. I have just four weeks — not nearly enough — in which to learn as much as I can *in situ*, and tally my impressions. (How dare I?) I'm not even *skimming* the surface, and have zero qualifications upon which to make judgements. (How dare I?) I'm an ordinary person. (Duh.) From a privileged country. (The nerve.) I'm customarily as tolerant as they come. (What is happening to me?) I am usually a polite guest, and quiet, to boot, but I can't help myself: the pandemic violence is veritably obliging me to speak.

~

A few nights ago we happened into a bar of English-speaking drinkers. There was a smart British blonde, and a slightly drunk American — let's call him Brian — who, I later learned, had married a young Mexican woman with children. (Apparently it's not going well.) We met a Canadian couple who'd sold off everything and bought a place here three years ago. They live with six adopted dogs and one mother/ mother-in-law.

There were others, too. Talk ranged from Peyton Place-type gossip to politically charged discussions concerning crime, the Mexican police, and drug wars. Crime and Non-punishment, if you will.

"Do you know anyone here whose home *hasn't* been broken into?" Brian asked his fellow expats. No one did. The Brit said: "But there was no violence involved in *my* break-in." Okey doke. Guess that makes B and Es and thefts A-OK, then. (What is happening to me?)

One man — and oh, how easily this could have been us in a few years — had been stabbed. "But it was just a gang initiation," he insisted. "I was walking and these young guys passed me on a motorcycle at about 11:00 at night. They turned around, and I began thinking, *Oh oh… this could be trouble.*" Well, trouble it surely was: he was stabbed in the chest. "But it was just a gang initiation," he said again — perhaps to himself — and took a healthy swig of his Pacifico.

Just a gang initiation? The knife narrowly missed his heart! Come on, I'm a dyed-in-the-wool, give-'em-the-benefit-of-the-doubt type too, but this guy gives *bleeding heart liberal* a far too literal twist.

We've made margaritas on our patio for a Canadian dog rescuer and her partner, a European-born wildlife photographer who's lived in Mexico for thirty years and speaks Spanish like a local. I thought he *was* Mexican, all 6'3" of him. He's been an extra in both *Titanic* and *Troy*, and it's not hard to imagine him as a gladiator. He's had guns pulled on him umpteen times, in sites ranging from the parking lot at Señor Frog's to the mountains where he regularly photographs leopards, macaws, and other beasties. "I don't go out at night," he says.

~

The other times I've visited Mexico I've thought: *Ah, yes, at last. My heart has found its long way home.* I've considered how easily I could walk away from Canada's creature comforts and spend the rest of my years in a *pueblito*, living simply, eating tortillas and *frijoles*, speaking the language, earning just enough through writing or teaching to keep myself afloat. Now I'm rethinking that fantasy. If this *is* a test run, the experiment's "gone south" in a way I never imagined.

Yes, one must keep an eye out for sidewalk dog shit, crossing a street is potentially fatal, and noise bylaws are seemingly non-existent, but these annoyances are altogether a different *bolsa de gusanos* (bag of worms) than innocent children being caught in machine gun crossfire in broad daylight while enjoying a coconut on the beach with their families. ("The more we get together ...")

Make no mistake: I *am* a diehard liberal, but in this moment, in this city, Mexico has lost some of its magic.

And I must examine my own ideologies.

~

I've now been waiting four hours for a technician. I pile the newspapers and add the front pages to the file I began when I arrived: news and photos one cannot believe.

Mazatlán, you action-adventure movie, you bloody horror show, you lovers-on-the-*malecón*-watching-the-sunset romance, you city of whistling parrots and Pacifico tours and AK-47-wielding killers who get away and away: *ay ay ay*. I wanted so much to love you.

BACK TO THE GARDEN

IN ORDER TO FUNDAMENTALLY APPRECIATE A GARDEN, must one be a gardener? I believe so. I can understand and trust a woman (or man) who spends hours on a little stool, tweezing miniscule weeds from around the pea plants and sweet peas, happy with the task. Even humming. Who else could rationalize the loonie-sized blisters on palms from digging dandelions with a tool made for that very purpose, then the lunacy of saying to oneself: *Only five hundred more, then I'll stop.* (And then not stopping, after all.)

There are back pains. Garter snakes. The scissoring sun. Slugs big as your thumb...okay, *bigger* than your thumb. There is dirt, mud, and sometimes blood. There is the knowing that you will never "catch up" in your lifetime, and the understanding that no one would even notice your grand efforts, and the calm realization that *it does not matter.*

I've heard that Martin Luther was asked what he would do if he knew that tomorrow would be his last day on earth.

Apparently he said he would go out and work in his garden: I'm with Marty.

It is spring after a long winter, and I am on the Sunshine Coast caring for my friend Flo's acreage, including gardens, pets, and home. This is no ordinary property, this is 3.5 acres of pristine *park*, with numerous gardens, old growth Douglas fir, a gazebo, a natural pond *and* a constructed, goldfish pond — with a bridge, waterfall, and one Herculean frog. There are fruit trees, and great shoots of bamboo, and several species not among my prairie gardener's lexicon. I liberally water the new grass during these hot, dry days, as if its proliferation will ensure proof of my good caretaking.

I have planted leeks. I have picked and frozen rhubarb. I have chopped the weeds, fed them to their specific composter and rotated them daily. I've stirred the general composter with a pitchfork, then covered this with wire to keep pets and wilder predators out. I water the delicate new sweet peas with sun-warmed water from a watering can, and spray the hardy kale with one of the many water hoses that twist away from a central tap in multiple directions: a octopus-like thing.

I've long been attracted to gardens: my own, of course, but I also love to be walked around friends' gardens and hear them discuss what they've planted, and why. I am learning that if you *really* want to know someone, you should work in her garden. I have more than two weeks here, and although Flo is in faraway Maui, I believe I have never felt closer to her.

Now I see what she sees at dusk, when the frogs start singing, and she's compelled to return to the vegetable garden — to be sure she remembered to close the gate, water the garlic, or have spinach already picked for tomorrow's salad. I think of her as I stop to watch the cacophonous ravens dart across the yard — four today, like kids playing tag — or the parental robins, guarding the nest they've built in the gazebo. I hear the wind rush through the bamboo and think there's a ghost standing by. When I open the patio doors first thing in the morning and give Jake-the-dog's head a warm pat, I smell the moist, florid air, as Flo must. To tend a friend's garden — to be *entrusted* with it — is to form a bond unlike any other.

The earliest gardens were planted for practicality: food and medicine. Many of us still take greatest pride in how the work of our own hands facilitates settler-like self-sufficiency, but the sensory beauty, and even the *symbolism* of gardens cannot be ignored. "Early enclosed gardens symbolized the joys of paradise," I read, while inhaling the soporific scent of cut lilacs in a mason jar. For early Christians, gardens embodied the feminine in nature, virgin purity, and the womb "for the conception and growth of everything that lives."

It's all so interesting. I feel I could spend the rest of my years writing solely about gardens, or perhaps just about the gardens on this acreage. (I often think this way: I could never take another photograph, for example, and I would still have enough material to keep me busy — editing, grouping, using the photos in multi-media projects — for the rest of my life. At what point does one say *Enough*, and start concentrating only on what one already has?)

Being here, among these wondrous gardens and pacific animals — adorable, good-tempered Jake and Percy-the-cat, who is friendly enough when petted, but swipes with hummingbird-quickness when you take your hand away — I am slowing down. My normal heart-rate is returning. And I am starting to think again. I suddenly feel I haven't *really* been thinking for months.

Tonight I am also pondering garden decoration, commonly referred to as "yard art." The latter term connotes gnomes and flamingos, plastic whirly-gigs and Canadian Tire specials. I'm not thinking about those things. I am thinking about tasteful additions to one's yard. Made art. Found art. Gifts from friends.

Some may conclude that a garden resplendent with shrubs, flowers, rocks, water features, trees, and dragonflies requires no further embellishment. Isn't the natural beauty enough? Ah, perhaps. But consider how a simple pair of diamond or emerald earrings, a slim bracelet enhances *human* beauty. Moderation is key. I believe there is a place for well-chosen, well-placed yard art, as my friend has situated around her postcard-perfect landscape. I find art camouflaged beneath hostas, and balanced on logs and stones. It is underplayed, and thus each discovery brings surprise and delight.

Gardens, with or without art, are an expression of — and extension of — personality. Think of a manicured garden with an immaculate lawn vs. a wild English country garden. Consider shade gardens, hued predominantly in greens, with hostas, ferns, and lamium, vs. gardens that explode with colour — blossoms coming and going like summer guests, from the earliest tulips, daffodils, irises, volunteer heart's-ease and peonies to poppies, columbine, lilies, lupins, hollyhocks, monkshood, and sunflowers. I love the white flowers: woodland anenome, fragrant phlox. I'm attracted to anything that blooms white, except daisies, which have nearly undone me with their Napoleonic insurgence in three different gardens. Death by daisy. A daisy plague. A daisy chain-gang.

But I digress. Easy to do when musing about gardens, or walking *through* gardens. When we add yard art, our gardens become even more remarkable. Sometimes it has the function of expressing personal beliefs. It can commemorate people, places, or things. I know folks who place stones or shells from their travels around their gardens. Yard decoration can certainly be store-bought. It can be recycled, i.e.: an old iron bed frame, or a wheelbarrow, spilling with flowers. Personally I'm anti-wheel wagon in a yard. And anti-white-painted bike. And anti-cement blocks that look like footprints.

But when did this all yard-artifice begin? Perhaps at the beginning. Perhaps cave people plucked pretty weeds and stuck them among the stones in their "yards," or arranged sticks or piles of little bones into small sculptures. We create. We have always created. We can't help it.

In the Regency Era in England — think palatial homes and acres of lawn — wealth and standing were represented by statues, fountains, and flowers. Yard art. Much later, and closer to home, I imagine prairie pioneers found innovative ways to brighten their yards after they'd cleared the land, built the sod hut, fed the babies, and got the potatoes in the ground, even if this was accomplished merely through stuffing a handful of black-eyed Susans into a rusted tobacco can.

Another thought: perhaps the *true* art is not so much in the individual items, but in the groupings and the placement of the whole. Perhaps the arrangements of multiple objects are really a kind of installation art.

This afternoon I strolled around my friend's gently hilled and generously treed acreage with a camera, snapping *art* that caught my eye. Some made — perhaps by her offspring, perhaps by herself. Some purchased. Some that looked antique, expensive, and elegant. The painted stones inspired by aliens and Munch's *The Scream* made me chuckle. I discovered bunnies that looked rather frightening, and a turtle that appeared it might move. I loved the simplicity of a single green rock set on a log bench. There's a happy gargoyle. West Coast art on the exterior walls. Each time I step into the garden, I see something new, and feel richer.

What I know about gardens is that it is okay to weep for beauty within them. It is okay to draw blood on arms and legs where blackberry bushes have whipped. It is just fine to stop and lift your face to the sky, close your eyes, and feel the sun upon your skin. Don't believe this is time wasted. Don't believe this is not important. On the contrary, this, my friends, is everything.

WHAT I LEARNED ABOUT LIFE AT THE END OF THE WORLD

FOR THE FIRST FEW HOURS I THOUGHT HER NAME WAS *Sigrud*. It is *Sigrun*, and we met in the coastal village of Salema, Portugal. The fit sixty-two-year-old Dane has lived in Salema — a particularly brilliant jewel in the 200-kilometre-long treasure box that is the Algarve — with her husband Jørn for the last thirteen years. Together they managed Pension A Maré, the privately owned guesthouse that sits like a blue-trimmed crown on the hill above the bus stop; a mere hop, step and long jump from the sprawling white sand beach. A few fishing boats bob on the viridian Atlantic — they're all that separates this southwestern tip of Europe from Africa.

Sigrun and Jørn no longer oversee A Maré, but it was our good fortune that they happened to be "filling in" for the current manager during part of our stay. Guests in A Maré's *sans*-kitchen suites are served breakfast in the communal dining room. The windows open to shocking sunshine; a constant breeze keeps temperatures bearable in this small fishing village. Whitewashed townhouses, an abandoned and almost-finished condo complex, restaurants, and small businesses stagger up Salema's hillsides. The steep slopes are bisected by cobblestone lanes only the brave or the foolish actually flip-flop up and down.

We had booked an A Maré apartment *with* a kitchen, but on the morning of day two I crashed the communal breakfast scene in a sheen of sweat. I was glistening from a ninety-minute walk/run — and ecstatic about the secret beach I'd discovered, the challenging cliff I'd climbed; ecstatic, really, to be alive — and the water cooler called.

A few guests were enjoying cold cuts, cheese and croissants, including Eystein, the young Norwegian who'd welcomed us to the guesthouse upon arrival. "The key's probably in the door," he said. "Ours was." And sure enough. We were agape at the view from our balcony: aquamarine ocean, long, sheltered beach, an artful display of palms, cacti and other exotic-to-us vegetation. We would have five nights in this Rick Steves' recommended guesthouse. The amiable Seattle-based travel writer and TV host — whom we'd coincidentally and delightedly met in person at the I.P. Pavlova metro station in Prague, but that's another story — put this place on the map, so to speak. A framed photo of Steves hangs in a local grocer's store (the same shop where I was told that if I hadn't enough money for my items, I could make up the difference later), and we worried we'd be rubbing shoulders exclusively with Canadians and Americans. This was hardly the case.

In the dining room, I filled my water glass and apologized to Jørn for my profuse sweating. "Don't apologize," he said, "it's natural." Then Sigrun introduced herself and asked if I would like to hike with her the following day. If so, I was to be at her house at 8:00 a.m. My partner, G, was also welcome. I did not even consider refusing; G hesitated only a little.

~

I am a fast walker, and, after twenty years of running — and early menopause — have become a slow runner. G is a slow walker and a fast runner. We agreed to meet in the middle as we left for Sigrun's house, just a few kilometres away. She was ready. Her wiry little dog — a Portuguese rescue — was eager to get going, too.

The three of us set out west at a good clip and were soon on a broad hilltop overlooking the salt-shaker village of Figuiera. Wind turbines wavered in the hazy distance. I wanted to get a sense of this particular place. I wanted to know everything. Was that aloe vera, or agave? (Agave.) Were there snakes here? (Yes, but it was the scorpions you had to be careful of — the smaller ones, not the large ones.) What was it like to manage holiday rental apartments? (She ironed sheets; enough said.)

The capital is a four-hour bus ride from Lagos, itself about twenty-five minutes via local bus from Salema. My introduction to Lisbon had been a happy one. We had just come from there, and found it magical — a sort of European sister to San Francisco, with its hills and trams, its ocean and disparate personalities. It was vibrant, historic, and had an easy-to-navigate metro system. I imagined Sigrun visited often. "I was last there in 2004," she said. Ah. My new companion was a singular woman indeed.

Sometimes we walked silently, as serious walkers often do. One must allow time to "take it all in," without comment, without feeling the need to converse. The popular expression is to "live in the moment." This is when you hear the wind, and note the scuttle of insects and reptiles in the dry grass. Colours announce themselves and beg comparisons: the cliff red as new potatoes. The sky enlarges, as does the sea. You feel the earth beneath your feet, and become aware of the shapes of stones.

After a time, Sigrun said, "Soon we'll be at the Roman road." We'd turned south off the road that leads through Figuiera and continues all the way to Sagres. "Two thousand years old." I imagined togas. Sandalled Caesars and Helens ghosting next to me. "What about that?" G asked, motioning to a stone wall that seemed to have no *raison d'être*. "No," Sigrun said, "that would be more recent." *Recent* here could translate as hundreds of years. Canadians that we are, G and I must often remind ourselves of that.

"This is like Eden," I said, noting the lemons that hung like tasty decorations on the trees. I asked Sigrun to identify the trees: olive, almond, fig. She pulled an almond off a sweeping branch. "You can eat them," she said. "Just crack them with a rock." She demonstrated, and G and I sampled the nut. Delicious. G asked: "What about the figs?" "They're are all privately owned," Sigrun explained. "You can help yourself to a few, but you can't gorge yourself on them."

We continued walking. It was getting hot, and I wished I'd not forgotten my cap. The little dog hopped along at our heels, oblivious to the climbing temperature. "I'm going to show you one of the secret beaches," Sigrun said. "There may be people without clothes on there." I couldn't resist telling her that this was the place I had discovered yesterday on my exploratory walk/run. A British couple — with three dogs — had met me on the trail that led to a narrower trail, then to the beach. I'd looked up the imposing cliff to the ruin on top. "Can one get up there?" I'd asked the pair. "Yes, there is a trail. Only the first bit is difficult." A few foot-holds up, I yelled back to them that if they discovered a dead Canadian later that day, my partner was staying in Salema.

I scrambled through blood-drawing brambles, grasped weeds I prayed were well-rooted. I grunted and climbed and scraped my way to the pinnacle, and the rest of the world fell away beneath the sandstone cliffs: there was only me and the large, blue hypnotizing eye that was the ocean off southern Portugal in August. *Come to me*, it seemed to say. *And you will be happy forever.* I dared not get too close to the edge.

We climbed down. "Wow," G said, as we took off our shoes on the boulder-strewn and bather-less beach. Camel-coloured sand. Someone had left a boogie board, apparently for communal use. Among many couples I know, one partner loves nothing better than to spread a towel on a beach and stay for hours, and one can hack that for about twenty-five minutes: G would be back to this beach before day's end.

"No one here yet," Sigrun said. "No nudes." I asked if she ever came to this beach to swim. She shook her head. "I'm an old nurse. I prefer people with a few clothes on."

We made our way home via the cliff, and learned where a large flat rock, partially hidden in an alcove of bushes, overlooked the ocean and would be "a great place to watch the sun set and have a glass of wine, if you're feeling romantic," Sigrun said.

I had finished all my water, and G's was gone too. A shower was going to feel divine at the end of this. Before we parted ways, our new friend asked: "Do you want to hike with me to Sagres tomorrow? It's a long one, but so beautiful. You'll need to bring a backpack with food." I had planned to visit Sagres the logical way: via bus. I wanted to see where Prince Henry the Navigator set the courses for explorers during the Age of Discoveries. One couldn't be this close to "the end of the world" and not actually experience it. I also wanted to go on an exploratory run with G the next day, but I knew he would be in beach mode for the rest of the holiday — the tail end of six glorious and economical weeks in Europe, centred on a house and car exchange we'd arranged with a French couple from the Alsatian village of Phaffans (but that is another story). "Okay," I said. "Sure!"

"We'll leave at eight again," Sigrun said. "Before it gets too hot." It would be seventeen kilometres. Or so. "I'll take a phone," she said, "and Jørn will pick us up."

Considering the challenging terrain and the heat, I expected we might be back by noon. Still lots of the day left for myself. This was important, because I'd been hoping for some kind of epiphany on this trip. I'd turned fifty a few months earlier, and after three decades of fulltime writing, ten literary books that caused little-to-no stir, some recent, wrenching sadness, and a family that was fully independent and far away, I felt I'd arrived at that mythical, undesirable, ennui-ridden place: the crossroads. Portugal, I hoped, would deliver me.

"Thanks," I said. Then Sigrun took the trail back to her home among the trees, and G and I scuffed down the hot streets of Salema back to our apartment, where we grabbed large handfuls of grapes right off the trees and washed them down with white wine.

~

We didn't go to Sagres; we went beyond. We hiked *sans* dog (too far for him), and *sans* G (too far for him) for eight hours, with one stop "to take a little bread" on a plateau, one coffee in a just-opening-for-business café several beaches from Salema, and two Diet Cokes (me), and one coffee (Sigrun) at a tourist-packed restaurant in Sagres with a killer view of the water.

One learns much about one's companion during a day-long hike, and I realized that this is what I love most about travel: meeting the interesting people who are put in my path. Sigrun and I shared stories about our families, our work, and the meat of our lives. Joys and regrets were covered. Hopes and fears.

After one breathtaking *From Here to Eternity* beach after another came into distant view, then fanned out beneath us, then slapped beneath our feet, I was reminded that sometimes we are more open with strangers than we dare to be with longtime friends and family. Sigrun told me about her childhood on the Faro Islands, and how hard her young, widowed mother worked to raise five children on her own. My hiking partner delighted in her single grandchild, Ida, who lives in Copenhagen. Sigrun showed me where she had watched fishermen struggling to haul a giant Portuguese man-of-war into their small boat — a vessel dwarfed by the lethal creature. She cursed the young hippies who "did their business" along the trail and left it, rather than digging a latrine and burying it. "I've stepped in human shit," she said. "It was awful."

At one stretch we had to beware of the shepherd's dog — a large one, Sigrun said, and very threatening. We carried rocks in our hands, but there were no signs of the sheep, shepherd, or Beowulf.

For a brief while, we linked into an actual marked trail, the Via Algarviana. "I prefer to make my own way," Sigrun said. And I understood completely, even if it meant occasional backtracking and the odd admission that one "doesn't have a clue" where one is. Terrain is rarely static: paths grow over, flowers die, colours change.

At one point, past Sagres, I realized how burned my shoulders were and slipped my long-sleeved running shirt over my tank top. I felt like a pillar of salt. Like a cow-lick. Almost completely wasted and dry as the skull of a coyote.

It was an extensive, arduous, desert-scorching, tangled, slip-sliding, scratch-and-burn way to the end of the world. The rewards were the vistas: that blue water that turned to turquoise, turned to green, and at times became translucent. It made one want to lie down and die in it, or at least rest for a year or two. The rewards were the conversations.

Before we reached the lighthouse at Cape St. Vincent, the *true* end (historical Sagres is a teaser), as it is the most southwestern tip of Europe, Sigrun dialled Jørn and said we were already there. A small lie, but one that put us into double-step mode for the last few kilometres. And how amazing, way out there, to see a kid on a longboard. How anachronistic to learn that we could buy a beer at the end of the world. Or a postcard. Or a hippie dress. Who *were* all these people?

Sigrun pulled me away from the souvenirs — I only wanted to look — and said: "Out there, *that's* what *really* matters." The cliffs dropped seventy-five metres, almost straight down, to the broiling Atlantic. Imagine climbing into a ship not far from here, waving goodbye to your loved ones, and setting out for brave new worlds. Imagine the bracing wind as land disappeared and waves rocked your vessel senseless, sails slapping so loudly you had to shout to the man right next to you.

I had Sigrun take a few photos of me against the royal-blue ocean and sheer cliff landscape, my hair whipping around my head like Hydra. Some fools went right out onto the cliffs for photos. "Do many die?" I asked Sigrun, while I watched a tourist balance precariously. A gust of wind. A slipping rock. It would be fast. She said that fishermen climbed out on the cliffs and embankments all the time, and yes, there were deaths.

It had been a long day, a tremendous day, and now Jørn was coming, and somehow it seemed right not to linger too long at our destination. It felt like looking at the sun, or witnessing a miracle. Maybe they're the very same thing.

I was burned and nicked and bleeding about my legs. I could have drunk my weight in water. And I became philosophical, out there on the promontory among the other tourists and the fervent wind. It seemed that the long hike was an apt metaphor for life. You struggle, you rest, you thirst, you are sated, you are grateful. You do it all again.

RUNNERS

My high school boyfriend remains a dear friend. Rob and I started dating when I was fourteen and parted ways during my eighteenth year, some time after I'd left Meadow Lake, Saskatchewan to study journalism arts at the Southern Alberta Institute of Technology in Calgary. I saw Rob not long ago, and he revealed that what has stuck with him over the years is that I always run from A to B. Yes. I run. I am now fifty-one years old, and I enjoyed an hour-long run this very morning through the sunny streets of Ladysmith and in the shade provided beneath Douglas fir, western red cedar and other giants on the Holland Creek Trail. Two weeks ago I surprised a large black bear on the path. Two months ago I tripped on a root and my knees were sewn up to the tune of fourteen stitches. I was running again the next morning. The day I can't bolt will be a sorry day indeed.

~

I began dedicated running on January 1, 1993. I had quit smoking the night before. I had been an off-and-on smoker since I was fifteen, and can remember when a pack cost fifty cents. When I got pregnant, I was definitely off. Young children: off. When I started working as a radio advertising copywriter for two rock and roll stations in Saskatoon, I was definitely *on*. Mostly I smoked because it gave me an excuse to pause. Mostly I smoked because I loved to pretend I was a 1940s movie actress. A sophisticate. It was more than a little about the aesthetic of holding that Number 7 Extra Light King Size. Of *brandishing* it. It was a kind of drama.

When I stamped out my final cigarette and committed to getting fit, I went all in. I rather quickly increased my distance (from one block to ten kilometres), and my extra weight dripped off. I lost twenty-five pounds so rapidly, it damaged my gall bladder and I had to have it removed.

I have been so serious about running, I went under the knife for a reduction mammoplasty. A breast reduction. Running an average of fifty kilometres a week with D cups had quite literally been a bloody chore: the straps of my running bras quarried into my collarbones. I was grooved and scarred. I saw a plastic surgeon, explained that I was a runner and showed him a photo of myself in an orange bikini, taken in the privacy of my garden. *You really* do *run a lot*, he said. I removed my shirt. He confirmed that I was an excellent candidate for surgery. He whipped out a measuring tape and marked two dots on my clavicles. He measured again, lower: *This is where your nipples will be.* Oh, my. He explained how he would fold the skin. *It's a matter of darts*, he said. *Like sewing*, I said. *Yes, just like that.* I asked if this would be like getting a haircut. *Can I bring in a photo of what I'd like? No*, he said, *it's not like that.* The surgery was a success — though I think he could have gone two cup sizes smaller.

Why all this running? I offer only theories. It beats down the demons, for one thing. Childhood trauma, melancholy, depression, loneliness, guilt. When you're struggling for breath, it's hard to dwell on your anguished spirit. Running's also the antithesis of sitting at a desk. It's hard work, and I believe in hard work, of *all* sorts. Protestant work ethic, perhaps. Or I could blame my Grade One teacher who taught her charges this little ditty: *Work before play, work before play ... that is the way to stay happy all day.* My parents are diabetic, and I'm determined not to go there. Running keeps me healthy and in reasonably good shape. It's proven a super way to explore new territory. My sport of choice is a go-anytime/anywhere activity, and all I really need for it are an hour a day and decent shoes.

～

In Saskatoon, I lived near the riverside Meewasin Valley Trail. In my home city I rarely missed a day of running between January 1993 and August 2007. I used to track the changes in the river, in the leaves. I ran with music, or without. With a dog, or without. I ran north, or south. Out-and-backs, or loops. I was intimately familiar with bridges and wind gusts. My son, cycling along beside me when he was thirteen, said: *Mom, for the amount you run, there should be nothing left of you.* My frosty face appeared on the front page of the *Saskatoon StarPhoenix* on December 22nd, 1998, when the temperature was in the mid to low -20° Celsius range. At times I was thin as a stick.

Then: life as I knew it changed. I initiated a separation, moved to a village, and endured an excruciatingly lonely existence that I felt must be my penance for abandoning my family. I always say it like that. Not *I left my husband,* but *I left my family.* My friends. My home, and the garden with heritage peonies and ferns, a bounty of pink and purple lupins, a trilling waterfall, a lacy green vine embracing the six-foot privacy walls. Oh, haven. Oh, flagstone path to the red garden shed, where I painted *S.L* and *T.L.* inside a heart and doomed it with that most doom-able of words: *Forever.* Oh, Muskoka chairs beneath the French lilac: I still miss you.

I blew everything right the fuck up.

What I left in the city: myself. And everything I'd known for the last twenty-four years. There was a woman and there was a cliff. She raced for it blindly.

～

In the village that followed, I was often a wretched beast. I wound the bed covers tightly around my shrinking self.

I longed for an intervention...

One day, Jackson the redbone coonhound — my best running partner — ate my car interior. A few months later he ate it again. Jesus. My melancholy was manifesting in my dog. Jackson found a new family, with children to play with, and acres of freedom.

It was November again, and everyone was saying goodbye.

~

I met a man on the popular virtual dating site Plenty of Fish; my profile name was *lovesthewoods*. We conversed online for weeks. He lived in Edmonton — a teacher who ran marathons. He had played in the Western Hockey League. Loved card games. His teenagers lived with their mother. He met my requisite six-foot minimum height requirement, and knew how to use a semi-colon. He was super-competitive, like me. We were a near-match in age. He read Canadian books. Had a sense of humour. Was decidedly not crazy. He would push me to run harder, faster, longer. A trainer *and* a boyfriend in one handsome package. A good man.

I knew my parents would adore him.

We lived provinces apart, but late December 2009 found me in High River, Alberta to house-sit and dog-sit for my Cancun-vacationing brother Kirby and his wife Laurel. At the end of January my online sweetheart and I decided to meet in person. *Because soon I'll be back home,* I e-mailed, *seven hours away, instead of three and a half.*

January, blizzarding. Bone-snapping cold, like a childhood winter in Saskatchewan. I packed the white German shepherd into the back of my sister-in-law's Subaru Outback, filled the tank, bought a lottery ticket, steered north. Surrealism: the hard-grained, blowing snow; the map of uncertainty; the man at the end of the highway, whose voice I'd not yet even heard.

I stopped in Leduc, let Gunner out for a pee. I intended to buy some new underwear and pajamas before the rendezvous. This potential life partner had invited me to pack a bag, just in case. *If you feel uncomfortable at all or don't like anything about me, please feel free just to turn around and drive back. But just in case, why don't you bring clothes and what you need for a few days' stay?*

I raced into a strip mall, grabbed a pair of black and white paisley pajamas at Giant Tiger. Flannelette. There was low-end lingerie on the racks, but even after a breast reduction, lingerie always made me feel ridiculous.

We were meeting in a downtown riverside park at 4:00. I didn't know Edmonton, and I was terrified of city driving, speed, slick streets, and smashing my sister-in-law's car. I navigated rush-hour traffic and one-way streets. I missed exits, pulled over to ask strangers directions. All I knew was that I had to find the blessed park and not invite bad karma by arriving late. I cursed my own superstitions.

Finally the sign: Dawson Park. He was standing outside his red convertible, against a backdrop of snow-weighted branches.

You are very pretty. His first words. It was -25°C. We unleashed Gunner, set out for a valley hike. G took my mittened hand after ten minutes; it was truly all I required. When the cold finally beat us, I followed his tail lights home.

~

We went to Jasper twice.

Spent a summer in Middle Lake, where gardening and home repairs and cribbage defined the days. I launched

Listen, Honey, a short-story collection, from the back deck. He made jam of the bountiful raspberries, ran like fire in the dry summer heat.

We blended families and played card games at the Greig Lake cabin. Fished at McFee Lake, Saskatchewan, and tanned on the panoramic beach at Waskesiu National Park.

There was a Hornby Island acreage for writing, running, connecting with artists, and learning we two should never share one kayak again.

A hot month in Mazatlán with dentistry, gun shots, and boogie boarding.

You do not know me / well enough to believe / I could realize the rest of my calendar / on the filthy beach / watching the chase game of waves.

The awful all-inclusiveness of Varadero, and the warnings of a Santeria priestess in Havana.

～

We moved.

Sechelt, British Columbia required a high school teacher with his credentials and experience. He went first, found us a Pan-Abode log house to live in, metres from Georgia Strait. *You won't believe it,* he said. Right in front of the house, he caught a salmon that could feed us for days. Kiwis and grapes dangled like jewels from vines around the deck. There were kayaks for our use. *You really won't believe it.*

Pack. Clean. Garden. Organize. My son visited in those final days in Edmonton, and we did what we do: hiked, biked, explored. My mother visited. My family, coming to say farewell to their vagabond again.

I loaded my own Subaru Outback and headed for the hills, over the hills, white-knuckled through the mountains and Vancouver, all the way to Horseshoe Bay. I sensed a fresh collective energy at the ferry queue. Joy. A woman noted my packed car, boxed bikes on top, and asked if I was moving to the Sunshine Coast. *Yes*, I said, *this very day*. Without any inducement, she bought a book from the back of my car.

Surely this was Shambala. Not even arrived, but every cell in my body vibrated, alerting me that I was getting close.

To what?

To where you need to be. To where you will *be. Now, and possibly forever.*

~

Living alongside the tides, waking with the waves, watching tugs make their daily log boom hauls, spotting a pod of killer whales from my desk. The sunroom swallowed the light in great gulps. I gulped it, too.

How did I live before?

A week or two in, I rummaged through my small wooden chest of business cards. Remembered a lotus, a dragonfly, flowers. Tattoos.

Flo? It's Shelley Leedahl. We met in Bali in 2009 ... I was with my adult son. I've moved to Sechelt!

~

Flo was instantaneously confidante, therapist, miracle, best friend. We took long hikes into the rainforest each Monday. The ropes of our lives intertwined. Each the mother of an adult son and daughter. Her son and my daughter are gay. I admired how she parented; her friendships with her children mirrored my own. We were gardeners. Dog-lovers. She taught me which was laurel, which salal. The Douglas fir, western red cedar, and twisty arbutus were as exotic to me as Cambodia would be.

There was also weekly guitar playing and singing with male friends. My blue binder spilled with new pop and folk songs. I fed a neighbour's chickens and gathered eggs for a month. A sign on the board by the mailboxes warned that a male cougar was recently spotted. I learned the names of the ducks — harlequins and common mergansers, surf scoters and buffleheads. I recorded new birds in my Saskatoon-begun bird book: black oystercatchers, glaucous and Bonaparte's gulls. I loved best the small, dark-eyed juncos and the family of bald eagles that nested on my temporary street.

I possessed a handful of new writer friends: poets and essayists, novelists and bloggers. I met an old pal of Joni Mitchell's. My partner was right: I couldn't believe my life in this place. I played guitar for his students at our house and no one was embarrassed to sing. I kayaked with leaping salmon. We crabbed. We caught flounder each time we dropped a hook.

And we ran: up to the airport; around Sechelt, Roberts Creek, and Gibsons; and out past Porpoise Bay Provincial Park.

I was the closest I'd been to happiness.

Then we left.

~

We were always moving. Back in Edmonton, we were either literally running — up to twenty-five kilometres on the best days — or planning our next escape.

Distraction was my mantra.

I began a poetry manuscript titled *Go*.

And often I went back to High River, where my brother was bravely and graciously enduring the final months of his years-long battle with multicystic mesothelioma of the peritoneum; we'd both somehow been exposed to asbestos as children. Playing in an attic? That's my guess. My tumours had been benign; Kirby's were malignant and malicious. I ran around High River listening to Lucinda Williams on my iPod. I cried into the autumn wind and mentally revised an obituary. I gave my brother massages and led him on meditations: *You're floating on an air mattress at the lake… the hot sun's on your back… you hear gulls overhead, happy children on the beach…*

My brother's death was the hardest thing I've ever survived.

I ran for my life, trying to pound death, unhappiness, the explosion in Saskatoon, the monotony of laundry, and two-eggs-with-toast breakfast routines into the pavement. I couldn't get far enough away.

I arranged a house and car exchange with a couple in the Alsatian village of Phaffans, France. We frequently Skyped and e-mailed; by the time they retrieved us at the airport in Basel, Switzerland, Chulita and Alain already felt like old friends. G and I got their Mercedes for a month, and they got my dog-clawed Subaru.

My high-school French proved insufficient in rural France. I ran to the *boulangerie* in the next town, Roppe, and asked for a *ticket* instead of a croissant.

We were living a dream, but as a couple we were swiftly unravelling. We infuriated each other on road trips because he was nervous driving and I was the anti-navigator. The wine tasting was great fun in Eguisheim — and all the other Alsatian "heims" — but there were too many tears in Strasbourg, where we never did locate our B and B on Rue de Bitche, and we didn't speak for two days in the aftermath.

Our map included Lucerne in the rain, and nights at another sister-in-law's ground-floor apartment in Aarau, Switzerland; my third visit, each time with someone new, each time a hike to the drinking fountain at the top of the wooded hill.

The TGV (Train à Grande Vitesse, or high-speed train) zipped us from Belfort to Paris for night cycling, the Impressionists, Pigalle strippers, and "Did you drop this ring?" gypsy scams all along the Seine. We ran past Diana's memorial and through Luxembourg Gardens, but we fought in the metro, arriving. We fought more in the monsoon-like rain.

In Germany we stole a few hours in Freiburg, with its cyclists and street canals and oompah-pah spirit. We ran in the Black Forest near Freudenstadt, and soaked up the edenism-hedonism of the Friedrichsbad spa in Baden-Baden.

And sometimes we argued a little less.

Prague was beery, well-explored, laced with easy-to-navigate trams and metros, a current of tourists on Charles

Bridge and at Prague Castle. At every corner, at least one wanderer bent quizzically over a map. But for me, Praha was all about art. I shot architect Frank Gehry's Dancing House from several perspectives. Professional artists and enterprising drunks broke into spontaneous street shows. We began to recognize David Černý's provocative sculptures: outside the Franz Kafka museum, two gyrating, mechanical men urinated into a pool shaped like the Czech Republic: *Piss.* At the intersection of Husova and Skorepka in Staré Město (Prague's Old Town), a tiny bearded figure dangled suicidally from a rooftop; Sigmund Freud in *Man Hanging Out.* I spent a day alone at the DOX Centre for Contemporary Art and wished I was young enough for a do-over: my next life would be all about art school.

We made a pilgrimage to red-roofed Český Krumlov — its old town a UNESCO World Heritage Site — and booked into Hotel Zlatý Anděl, the same hotel Kirby had enjoyed years before. We lifted heavy glasses to his memory. G bought three ornate steins from a shop along the winding, cobbled streets; I bought postcards at the Egon Schiele Art Centrum, a purple pashmina scarf from a boutique, Mary Janes from a Chinese grocer.

There was a cockroach in the stairwell of our apartment in Lisbon's Alfama (where we slept in separate beds), but this oldest city in western Europe was especially good to us. On a long morning run, we happened onto Casa Pastéis De Belém and the famous custard tarts — *pastéis de nata* — burst in our mouths. We couldn't get over how cheap and delicious the wine was, how amazing the fish, how hypnotic the fado, especially when sung by those who one could believe had lived long enough to have experienced the melancholy of which they sang. We rode the fabled street cars and skipped the cathedrals. There was a big deal made of a minor infraction (beach drinking, no I.D., and a siren-screaming, speed-wild, cop-show-style ride from Estoril to Lisbon in the back of a police car), and finally summer's conclusion in the glorious Algarve.

~

In Edmonton we wore out numerous pairs of running shoes and hung the "dead" ones from garage rafters. Before I met G, I got more exercise than anyone I knew. He always went the extra mile. He sprinted up cliffs. He ran a respectable marathon in Red Deer and I didn't embarrass myself there in my first half-marathon. We ran in snow and sleet and temperatures that should shear human skin.

We discussed civic politics and Oilers' draft picks. Went to plays. Won turkeys, ground beef, chicken, pork and pot roasts at the Norwood Legion's Friday night meat draws. We were one canoe snug inside another (our best thing) on the worn blue couch as we transported to *House Hunters International* locales. We took a ride on a murder/mystery steam train between Big Valley and Stettler, Alberta. We had *Mad Men*, *Breaking Bad*, and a DVD box set of *Nip/Tuck*. We hosted poker parties, played miles of cribbage, and became addicted to the board game Settlers of Catan.

Eventually he stopped watching movies with me. He did not garden. Or sing. Or do housework. And I could only get so excited about hockey.

Often, near the end, it was quiet. I stayed until the silence was deafening.

I stayed almost four years.

~

We never stopped running. But at some point — perhaps on Ada Boulevard in Edmonton, perhaps on the river valley trails — he started running far ahead and did not check to see whether I had in fact died or was still trying my damnedest to follow.

~

For some of us, happiness is a constantly moving target. We run as hard as we can, try to chase it down. We never quite get there. Would we even recognize it if we did?

EGÉSZSÉGEDRE

~ 1 ~

I BOARD A PLANE FOR HUATULCO, MEXICO AT THE Edmonton International Airport. A dark-haired stranger in a blue pin-striped shirt takes the seat directly in front me. I hear him speak to the flight attendant, think he is a French businessman.

I am wild about flying. I always expect to read, and rarely do. I sometimes expect to crash and am not concerned, because I will survive. I will build a raft, but will not want to leave the island. Strength and athleticism: the sum of my confidence.

The geography changes colours and textures beneath me. Much of it is tan-toned, treeless. The landscape wrinkles like skin in a desert. So much territory left to inhabit. Do others consider this when viewing the world from above?

And what are those huge disc shapes pressed into the ground? Perfect circles, as if made by a goliath mathematical compass.

The woman beside me, from Fort McMurray, shares that there are seventy-five people onboard to attend a wedding. The bride is the loud one in first class, six seats ahead. She's obviously indulged in some serious pre-tanning. My neighbour says she feels she always has to defend Fort McMurray. *It really is a great place to live.* She orders $95 worth of duty-free make-up.

I am in awe.

I consider the back of the head of the stranger before me. What's going on in there? He uses the vacant seat next to him to prop his laptop. I am given to fancy and folly. A fleeting, unbidden seed of a thought, 35,000 feet above sea-level: what if he and I — the only two passengers to board this SunWing vacation flight as soloists — were to connect? Absurd.

~ 2 ~

Once upon another journey, I met a woman named Flo. We first spoke during a layover in Taipei. Flo and her two friends had noticed my adult son and me in the airport, and said her friends — gay males in their fifties — were curious about the relationship between this older woman and her gorgeous young travelling companion. It was 2009. I no longer recall the dialogue verbatim, but knowing Flo as I do now, it may have been: *Hi. My friends — see those pervs sitting over there? — want to know if you two are lovers.*

We didn't see Flo and her travelling companions again until nine days later, on our final night in Sanur, Bali. Logan and I were on a drunken tear after more than a week of cultural, spiritual, and mother-son enlightenment. I felt we had begun the trip as two people who had forgotten who we were both as individuals and as family, and we were closing the trip with monumental appreciation for our shared experience, all things Indonesian, and humanity at large. On the final night, we found ourselves in a beach bar with Swedes, Irish, Australians, more. Music pulsed, and one outgoing, likely my-aged Canadian, with vibrant insect and floral tattoos — *pollinators* — on her limbs, was encouraging others to dance. *Hey, it's you again!* I am not one who must be dragged toward a dance floor.

So where are you from? I shouted over Bob Marley's odes to joy: "Sun is Shining," "One Love."

Sechelt, she said, and continued dancing.

I hazily placed Sechelt on BC's Sunshine Coast, near Gibsons. I'd never been to that part of Canada, but a dozen years earlier had published a juvenile novel concerning a quirky family from Gibsons who moved to Saskatoon in the cold heart of January. *Riding Planet Earth.* I'd grown up with Nick, Jesse, and Relic from *The Beachcombers* TV series and had always hoped that one day I, too, would lift a pint at Molly's Reach beside the scenic harbour.

I'm the town body-piercer, Flo said. There was something vaguely African and vastly graceful about the way she internalized the music, sinuous arms in motion as if impelled by a this-a-way-and-that-a-way breeze. When some women dance it's like they're making love to the world.

I live in rural Saskatchewan, I said. *A lakeside village of 300 souls, but I spent most of my adult life in Saskatoon, where Logan lives, and my daughter. I write books few people read.*

We should exchange cards, one or both of us said.

But we exchanged more than cards. When I moved to Sechelt with G, I reconnected with Flo and we became fast friends. I missed her when we moved back to Edmonton, and when she suggested a winter getaway to Mexico, I couldn't resist.

~ 3 ~

Over Bahías de Huatulco in Oaxaca. Southwestern Mexico. We sweep above thick treetops that look exactly like broccoli. Miles and miles of broccoli. Impenetrable jungle. A different Mexico than Mazatlán, Mérida, Puerto Vallarta and the less touristic *comunidades mexicanos* I've spent time in.

It is a rough landing. We bounce. Audible gasps are followed by scattered applause. The airport buildings have palapa roofs.

I disembark quickly, but there's a delay inside while the Customs' dog sniffs bags, and I must stifle my impatience. Some passengers change from jeans and jackets into shorts and sandals: I just melt. And pace as little as possible.

Finally we are allowed through the doors and there is my Flo, waiting and lovely in a sundress that accentuates her rainbow-coloured tattoo sleeve; another jungle. She'd arrived earlier via Vancouver. I apologized for the tardiness.

It's fine. I've only been here an hour.

I link arms with her — this need to *touch* those I love — and we step into the late-day sunlight, inhale the heady tropical perfume. It smells like a floral fusion, like Venezuela. And Honduras. A fragrance that is very nearly a taste. The climate is hot like Belize but not as oppressive as the Dominican Republic, not as wind-driven as Honolulu. Huatulco is all its own. We are almost swooped with the masses into one of the buses waiting to transport the wedding party and likely ninety-nine percent of the other passengers toward the deluxe all-inclusive resorts just south of town. *We're not part of the party*, I tell the tour guide. And then it happens: that old friend hyper-sensitivity kicks in. The guide's white shirt turns phosphorescent. An unseen bird seeks his brother. It's almost as if I can feel the sun's individual rays as they grace my skin. Oh, magnolia heart. Senses hit overdrive, but my brain's not reconciled the *where* of me yet.

We're staying at Hotel Villablanca. A modest, sixty-room, Mexican-owned hotel between Santa Cruz and La Crucecita. Not on the beach. Affordable for a full-time writer and a self-employed body piercer. The guide points to a van.

The tall stranger is waiting there too.

~ 4 ~

In Edmonton I run several times a week. I run to the brink of collapse. I also swim laps like my life depends upon it: minimum two kilometres. I have a few good friends, an eight-hour-a-week job as a radio advertising copywriter for two rock and roll stations.

I share a pleasant home in an inner city neighbourhood with my partner, G.

Sometimes he finds me staring out the bedroom window into the garden, across the twist of electrical wires to the sky, and the alley, where I once startled a prostitute plying her trade. In the front yard, whilst digging weeds to prepare for sod, I unearthed a used hypodermic. Pin-prick. Months of testing and shots. Here the only birds are wearisome magpies, and that larger bird, the police helicopter. My favourite thing is to lie in bed alone and be quiet as smoke.

I wasn't always like this, but I have been for a very long time.

~ 5 ~

At the hotel's front desk I switch to vehement Spanish when I learn Flo and I will not be getting our ground-floor, poolside room as requested one month earlier. We get the room. It opens, impeccably, to our private patio and faces the lush courtyard: pool, palms, ferns, bougainvillea, and bird-of-paradise. Gulls pluck beetles off the water. A white-haired man with a chest incision scar — and the circumference of a pacemaker visible beneath his skin — splashes at the sporting birds.

Flo and I eat meat-heavy dishes — pork, beef, and chicken all on one plate — at the hotel's restaurant, then walk a little in the dark street. It is mostly empty and feels like the moon. An occasional taxi driver spots us, loops around, honks hopefully. *No gracias, solamente estamos caminando.*

We're just walking. We cross the palm-studded boulevard, to the better-lit side. My friend says: *These palms ... they've tried to make this look like California.* I have never taken a vacation with a girlfriend. It is peaceful and slightly awkward: Flo has articulated that she hopes we'll be good travelling partners. She says the things most people only think; I occasionally *do* them. We return to our hotel, pour cocktails at the patio table: Flo brought vodka, we'd purchased orange and peach juice at the nearby Super Che.

And there he is again, two rooms over at *his* patio table, focused on and illumined by his omnipresent laptop. The man from the plane. High cheekbones, the broad brow of a thinker. Something inherently vulnerable about his pretty mouth, the slightly hunched posture. A big man feeling small, I predict.

And here, friends, is the hinge. From this moment forward my lesser mechanics — logic and reason — crumble like rust.

Flo, I don't think that man is meeting anyone here. I think he's on his own. We should invite him to join us for a drink.

You go, girl.

I can be brazen. It is partly the result of a paternally inherited, gregarious personality. It is partly that one week will pass more quickly than a Mexican sunset, I am fifty years old, and time is collapsing. It is partly Flo's vodka.

Hello. You sat on the plane in front of me from Edmonton. My friend and I — I motion left — *are wondering if you'd like to join us for a cocktail.*

His name is Laszlo. He moved to Edmonton from Budapest four years earlier with his second wife and his son from a previous marriage. The current wife is thirty-three, and she left him two weeks ago. Missing in action. No note, no forwarding address, no idea why. This is a man in shell shock. His son will be eighteen in December.

I love that boy so much.

Laszlo has a small marketing company. He does not offer details and I don't press.

I don't really know what I'm doing here, he admits.

Flo smokes his cigarettes and makes us laugh.

~ 6 ~

I'd noticed the sign when we were leaving the airport: *Bienvenidos al Paraíso.* Welcome to Paradise. Indeed.

Every day is bejewelled in Huatulco. Flo, Laszlo and I walk into town. Flo, Laszlo, and I enjoy dinners together — pizza at the hippie place, La Crema, or fresh fish with rice and a suggestion of salad on the beach. Flo, Laszlo, and I on a different beach, exploring a new-to-us coral reef each day. Flo calls us her Sisters. She doesn't know I am surreptitiously looking for Laszlo the moment I awake. While eating papaya and mangos at breakfast. Sitting outside our room. Hungry away from him. Happiest, always, when he's near. But I expect nothing.

Tourist season has not officially begun, and the locals scramble for our patronage. I hire Venancio to take us along the coast in his boat, the Luz Fat. We invite Albertans Rhonda and Greg to come along. I know them. I lived next door to Rhonda's mother in Middle Lake, and Rhonda rented my house over the Christmas holidays a few years earlier.

We have snorkelling gear and a cooler full of beer. Venancio has limited English; he speaks mostly to me, in Spanish. He leads us out of the marina and points out the face carved in the cliff wall, the flying fish which are like flat stones skipped across water. We stop at superlative beaches to bake on the sand, to snorkel, to drink. I like the blue fish best, and the silver, circling schools. Hour upon hour, the day is as close to perfect as anything in recent memory. We spot sea turtles in the choppy waves and take photos of one couple mating. *Does that make you horny?* Flo asks in her convincing British accent. It's our shtick. We pretend to be *proper ladies*.

Venancio throws a fishing line from the bow and hooks a tuna fish; Laszlo pulls it up. We admire and return it to the sea. I am in hardcore love with the sun, the waves, the salt on my face. My white linen shirt pastes against me like a second skin. I trail my hand in the water. Jesus. I realize it's been far too long since I was awake.

On the Luz Fat we keep switching seats so everyone will have a turn in the front, where one can stretch legs and enjoy the supreme view. Laszlo and I spend much time in the primo spots, where it is a little dangerous: Venancio bumps across the water with such speed and force we laugh like children. We cannot stop. Soon it is impossible to look at Laszlo without fear of giving myself away. Too long I gaze, too deeply. I do it anyway.

~ 7 ~

Releasing baby sea turtles beneath the moon at Bahía Chahué: a conservation project involving marine biologists, government agencies, locals, and tourists to help the endangered little tykes — they look and feel like weightless scraps of leather — return to the sea before natural or human predators strike. After a long lecture in Spanish and a short translation in English, Flo, Laszlo, and I cup our hands and kneel on the still-warm sand alongside the others to let our babies go.

I kneel next to Laszlo. Neither of our turtles moves a flipper. I almost step on mine. Laszlo's starts in the wrong direction. I try to be in the moment: I am a woman on a dusky beach in southern Mexico, releasing a baby sea turtle beside the heart-shattered Hungarian I am trying desperately hard not to fall in love with. Nope, too surreal to process. I would make a miserable Buddhist.

We return much later that night when the crowds are gone and only lovers and drunk teenagers from the nearby nightclub pepper the extensive beach. The bright moon casts our increasingly cozy triangle in a kind of prolonged twilight and defies the time on my watch. We set our towels close together on the sand, and mostly the moon and the sea do the talking. Night has taken a mystical turn; it seems incredible that just hours earlier locals were jogging in slow motion through the thick sand, and a red flag advised against swimming. I feel giddy after a time. Do some unsuccessful cartwheels on the sloping beach. Flo dances. Laszlo smokes.

It gets so quiet, by and by, I think someone might kiss someone. It's anyone's guess.

But the moment passes, and in another hour we are flip-flopping toward the two-storey nightclub. A Cuban band plays on the main floor. Upstairs it's vibrating techno. We determine we're not dressed properly for either, and to Villablanca (with beer buzzes) we go.

Oh, little Miss Daring. I hug Laszlo goodnight like I mean it.

~ 8 ~

On the second-last full day, my sisters and I taxi to Bahía Maguey. We set our towels and drinks beneath the scrawl of trees at the end of the beach. An animal that might be a wild cat struts out of the jungle. I yell: *Last one in is a rotten egg!* and Flo bullets past on *is*. Another day that warrants a page in the book of my lifetime. In and out of the crystalline sea, as if the tides are also at work on us. Talking and not talking. All *mexicanos* here, save us. A man draws crowds with an enormous albino ball python draped around his shoulders. Take a picture of this. Take a picture of Flo kissing an iguana. Take a picture of families eating sandwiches on the beach. Take a picture of anchored boats bobbing in waves. Take a picture of heartbreak: the young man in dress shorts throwing a floral bouquet from the rocks when he must suspect no one is looking.

Flo is swimming again. Laszlo throws pebbles at me. I throw some back. I read him two poems from the literary journal *Grain*. He really listens. Then Flo flops, wet and sandy, onto her beach towel between us.

Surely, this sister must know.

~ 9 ~

Anything can happen on the last day of a vacation in paradise. Time still has no meaning. Flo, Laszlo, and I cab to Bahía Entrega, where a pelican sits like a sentinel on the barnacled rocks above the swirling, royal-blue water.

Pelicano. One magnificent specimen lifted off Greig Lake, Saskatchewan in June at the precise moment my little brother Kirby's cremains met the water in Hidden Bay. That bird put on the best show ever.

Before my beloved brother died, I had spent weeks in High River to help ferry him toward the river we all one day return to. Oh, Kirby. I was my best self then. It was the worst time. So much to say about this singular man. I am still too humbled to even begin.

Everything is in circles. It all comes around again, and feels like déjà vu. Perhaps there truly is nothing new under the sun, as Solomon stated in Ecclesiastes.

Flo, Laszlo, and I have packed swimsuits and snorkel gear. I stuffed a few *cervezas* into my bag. Our taxi driver stops so we can admire the view of the bay from the lighthouse. I look straight down the cliff. Sudden death. Zero iguanas.

A restaurant manager allows us to stash our knapsacks back near the kitchen because we will eat and drink at his establishment, furthest to the right, with sandbags serving as steps, for as long as this day lasts.

We don masks and snorkels and plunge into the water, kicking toward the point where the pelican sits with a patience I could never own. The Mexicans around us are mostly in lifejackets; Flo points out some entirely distinctive swimming. The snorkelling is decent. I see an eel but it's gone by the time I alert Flo. There's a smaller beach beyond the rocky outcrop. Like swamp things, we lurch from the water to flop onto sand that's clean and white as a page. Only one other small family of three at this oasis. A Mexican from the capital asks if his daughters, ten and twelve, can ask me some questions in English. The girls are so shy in their wetsuits. *Where. Do. You. Live? Do. You. Have. Children?*

After the English lesson the family swims back to the main beach. Laszlo is on his back on the sand, arms splayed at his sides, eyes closed. Already a much different man than the one who sat before me on the plane. Flo seeks partial shade in the trees. The sand's heat pulls the length of my body toward it. I lie several metres away from Laszlo, surreptitiously watch him sift the soft sand through his fingers. The sun presses us into the landscape. No boat noise, everyone else gone. Perfection.

After a time, Flo says: *I'm going back for something to eat.*

Okay, I'm going to keep snorkelling for a bit, I respond. Laszlo doesn't move. His broad chest and rib cage. Narrow waist in the "boy cut" suit. Long, muscular legs. The body of a one-time competitive swimmer — he was on the Hungarian National Swim Team, decades back — who's been blessed to retain his athletic shape. God, but it hurts to look.

I splash back into the ocean for some shallow snorkelling and, yes, a pee. Except for half an hour on his patio deck the night before — when Laszlo surprised by professing his attraction for me, and I confessed my own — we have not been alone together. I take a deep breath and kick to the depths. Hand-sized fish come close and skitter away. Approach, then scatter, as if they are as curious about this creature as I am about them.

Okay, girl. If anything is going to happen, it is going to happen now. Right there. On that steaming beach. Where his is the solitary body. He is the lone survivor of the shipwreck.

I adjust my suit straps, rake fingers through my hair. I perform my best mermaid: emerge, and head straight for him.

I lie next to him, face up to his face down. Nearly touching. I'm wet and salty, he drips with perspiration. Oh, skin-next-to-my-skin. Oh, holy mother sun. His beautiful lines. The landscape of muscle and bone. What poems I could make of him.

A few moments, just for breath-catching. And being. I grasp a handful of sand and slowly smooth it onto his broad back. Then another. An intimacy. Like we're already lovers. The entire world disappears when we lean in to kiss.

~ 10 ~

We arrange to sit together on the flight home to Edmonton, and our only option is to take the seats that do not recline. He squashes in against the window and I melt into him. When he traces my ear with his finger I know. When he draws on my inner arm. I have been starving. To be touched like this is for me akin to the miracle of respiration. We kiss for the next six hours. Sometimes we talk.

~ 11 ~

Back in our city, he is eight passports ahead of me in the Customs' queue: enough for each of us to gain perspective. His expressive brown eyes. He sees through me. We glance away, then lock eyes again. Shake our heads a little — *Thank you, God, for this* — lock hearts and gazes again. Better than words. Walls cave. I implode.

~ 12 ~

His son pulls up to the WestJet doors and we get into his Taurus. Laszlo says something in Hungarian. Kisses him. Edmonton's the coldest place on earth and my car's in long-term parking in Leduc.

The teenager drives.

That black Subaru, I say, *buried under the snow.* They ensure it starts, and Laszlo sweeps snow off my windshield. His hoody is pulled over his head, like a teenager.

Are you gonna be okay?

I have scribbled the smallest note on my slightly bent business card. Three monosyllabic words, and his name. I press the card into his jacket pocket.

Please, read it later.

~ 13 ~

Next day in central Edmonton, I tell G: *We have to talk.*

I start collecting boxes from Superstore and SaveOn. Every day for the next week more of me is folded into them. I use a black Sharpie, make bizarre juxtapositions: *Bathroom scale and Shell's magnets from around the world. Books I've written, plus Scrabble dictionary.* My dear friend Anna Marie has lent packing tape.

~ 14 ~

G says: *Why are you even still here?*

I will leave behind a library of books. Shelves. My piano. My inherited Queen Anne chairs and the mahogany bedroom suite I bought with more than one month's pay from my radio job. I leave art on the walls, the Muskoka chair I put together and painted teal blue. The new concrete birdbath. Some day I will return for the heavy black fire-pit my son artistically welded as a gift for me one Christmas ago.

There is so much dust. I vacuum again and again. If I must leave this man, I will leave him spotlessly. I open the cabinet beneath the kitchen sink. A large rag hangs over the water pipes. I tear it in half. Scrub the kitchen and bathroom floors as I always have, on hands and knees, like my paternal grandmother, who cleaned for wealthy families in Saskatoon. I scour doorknobs, the cutlery drawer. I clean beneath the stack of frying pans. How Stepfordian I've been. Four years of cooked breakfasts. Four years of white undershirts washed with a hint of bleach, dried for two minutes, hung on the clothes rack, folded, set back in the dresser beneath the ones already there.

My neck is beyond damp, my shirt plastered to my skin. When there's not a fingerprint left, I throw one half of the rag into the garbage. The other I hang back on the pipe to dry. A faded square of flannel. Black and white. Barely there paisley design.

~ 15 ~

Penultimate night with my partner of four years. *House Hunters International* is featuring three homes in Huatulco. *I taped it for you,* G says. *We can watch it together.*

There is Playa Santa Cruz, where the full moon rose over the hill of abandoned houses, hung there like an amulet, and we took photos that did not do it justice. There's the main square downtown — the *zócalo* — with its central gazebo, and old men smoking on orange-painted benches. And there, a medium shot at Bahía Entrega. The camera pans the beachfront, stops on the restaurant furthest to the right. I see the sandbags that serve as steps. So close in memory. And, unfathomably, right here in our living room. Surely this must mean something. Everything always means something.

Then a voice not my own inside my head says: *Shelley Ann, you make beautiful gardens and ruin beautiful lives.*

~ 16 ~

It is a strange thing to move in with a man before you even know if he has any allergies. You don't know his middle name, how he got to Canada, or whether he can cover his power bill.

You don't care.

For the second time in less than four years I hang my scant wardrobe in a foreign closet. I unload the boxes from my car, pile them into his basement. It will be weeks before I can find anything. I don't want to find anything.

There is only love now. Whole, like milk. Milk in Magyar: *Tej.* It sounds like my daughter's name, abbreviated: *Tay.*

~ 17 ~

Family fallout. My daughter is cool, my son downright frosty. He invested in his relationship with G, he says. Taylor loved the one before that. They have colluded, these children of mine. In their separate ways they mutually proclaim: *We'll not get close to any of your men again.*

My mother: *Eastern European! How do they treat their women?* I don't know, Ma, but I'm about to find out. My sisters hear it better. My sister-in-law in High River, widowed almost one year, will never be surprised by anything again.

Each time I speak to my parents on the phone, my father's same question: *What does this guy do?*

He loves me, Father. He outlines my ear with his tongue. He writes with his fingertips on the insides of my arms. He stands behind me on escalators and presses his body into mine. He calls me *Honey-honey. My love. Angel,* and *Naughty Angel.* He asks: *Are you real, Shelley? Can this be real at all?* And I cannot answer with certainty. We hold each other all night long. He looks at me, and does not stop, and this is worth more than gold stocks. I breathe on his back. I play with his hands. I massage his feet.

He is under-employed, I am a literary writer. We will be poor. We will eat frozen pizzas from Safeway and drink too much Diet Coke. So long, red wine at dinner. Farewell to buying every book I wish to read. We may well have to live in a dive.

I have not been loved in so long.

~ 18 ~

We sign up for the YMCA fitness centre with our two meagre cheque stubs and qualify for a subsidy. *Let me do the talking,* Laszlo says. *My accent. Sometimes they take pity on us guys.*

Side-by-side treadmills face the snowy outdoors. One end of the West Edmonton Mall rises above residential rooftops. I run faster and go further because I have been practising all my life. It is good to sweat beside him. To reach out and feel him there, soaking through his collared, pale blue T-shirt.

Now he's ready for the pool, and I'll ride the recumbent stationary bike. Twenty minutes later I can't wait another moment to see him. I stand above the pool, peer through the wall of glass. Oh, my heart. He looks and swims like an Olympian.

He spies me and sends a wet kiss toward the glass.

~ 19 ~

The son is the centre of his world, and soon I am also doting on this reticent, blue-eyed almost-eighteen-year-old. *How many eggs would you like for breakfast? How many pieces of toast?* My own children never knew this woman. Their ongoing joke is that they were the only kids in Grade One who had to make their own lunches. Oh, little independent darlings, wary now of their gypsy mother and her unconventional ways. Laszlo suggests I have lived my life backwards. The roaming, the relationships experienced now rather than during my early twenties, because I was already a mother then, and it was essential to get that exactly right.

The son gives me some new Hungarian vocabulary each day. *Szia.* Hi. *Jó éjt.* Good night. *Tiz.* Twenty. *Egészségedre* means "to your health," and we say it as we drink their Hungarian red wine in my stained-glass goblets. One evening Laszlo calls his son into our room and they laugh as I try to pronounce Hungarian phrases. We bond over umlauts.

~ 20 ~

The synchronicities. We both keep pennies in our mailbox. Love flower gardening, and are trying to overwinter geraniums. We both chipped a front tooth in a childhood diving accident and have not had said teeth repaired. We prefer an elegant Christmas tree, decorated in just one or two colours. We use reading glasses of the same strength: 1.50. Can't stand public nail-clipping. His cell phone's alarm ringtone is the same as my son's.

~ 21 ~

I take him to my company's Christmas party and the woman next to me whispers: *He's* so *good-looking*. Yes. He looks like he just walked off a movie set. He looks like a young Tony Curtis. In his black track suit with the white stripe, he looks like the Eastern European bad guy in a film featuring painful executions and car chases.

~ 22 ~

It is the one-year anniversary of my little brother's death. I have been living with Laszlo for three weeks now, gratefully. Passionately. Spiritually, too. He holds my hands over our breakfasts and dinners and silently prays before we eat. We have sung carols together in church. When he closes his eyes and bows toward his plate, private in his thoughts, my mantra begins: *Thank you for this man. I love this man. Thank you for this man. Oh please, give us time.*

His name has become my prayer. *Laszlo,* I say. *Amen.*

～

His grandmother dies in Budapest. He weeps like a child. I hold him tightly, stroke his back, whisper like any mother would.

Lover, brother, friend, soulmate, son. I have fallen so deeply down the well there is zero hope of safe return.

～

We plan an imminent move to BC. Sechelt, perhaps, where our sister is. I love my home province of Saskatchewan and have enjoyed my adopted province, Alberta, but the west coast is where I instinctually need to be. Laszlo will never have to suffer another bitter Edmonton winter. I will use my life savings to buy us a modest home. I obsess over online real-estate listings. We'll find jobs. Say we'll do anything. Work as gardeners, house painters. Commute to Vancouver. We really will do anything. Except live in a trailer.

~

I am not naïve. He is too fetching for me; beauty often courts trouble. His son may not be ready to be alone. The wife might return. A million things could shatter. A million. *Egy millio.*

If we have a hundred days I will be thankful. And if we go the distance I can die happy, at last.

~ 23 ~

My friends, I have not been truthful. I have always been like this. Always and exactly, just like this.

NOTES ON THE ESSAYS

Some writers have suggested that they write because they want more than one life — it is a purely selfish desire. I am greedy, too, but I identify most closely with the American writer William Goyen, who — in a 1975 interview for *The Paris Review* — suggested that "[Writing] is simply a way of life before all other ways, a way to observe the world and to move through life, among human beings, and to record it all...and to shape it, to give it sense, and to express something of myself in it." I'm not convinced it's possible to make sense of my life, but in writing down these few parts of the life I've lived, I at least make my best attempt.

I've previously published (or had broadcast on CBC Radio Saskatchewan) numerous essays that did not find their way into this book: pieces about the writing life, about birthing and parenting, about participating in international artist retreats, and about extremely personal matters, like the reduction mammoplasty I underwent in 2006 because

I have chosen to be a lifetime runner. The resultant essay, "Tits," appeared in *Slice Me Some Truth: An Anthology of Canadian Creative Nonfiction* (Wolsak & Wynn, 2011). It's bloody, and graphic, and decidedly too far afield from the content in this collection.

I thank Karen Haughian at Signature Editions for pursuing this project with me as my return address labels repeatedly changed between Alberta, Saskatchewan, and British Columbia. I am grateful to my wide and eclectic cast of family, friends, and partners for inspiration, and for ensuring, always, that life is anything but dull.

~

It is important to note that these pieces were written in *real* time; many places and situations have changed since they were penned, i.e.: "my husband" is no longer my husband, new highways have been constructed, and I have now been to Scotland. Some names have also been changed.

"Road Trip" — The song I referred to is, actually, "In the House of Stone and Light," by British musician Martin Page, released in his 1994 album of the same name. I made it to Scotland in 2004. The highway between Saskatoon and North Battleford is now double-laned.

"No Oceans, No Mountains, There's No Place Like Home" — I've always been a defender of the prairie landscape. Less dramatic than some provinces, yes, but all the beauty is here, too. You may have to look a little harder for it, but perhaps it's sweeter for the effort. An anecdote re: the 1992 film *Damage* (Louis Malle, director)...I posted a review on IMDb (International Movie Database) which resulted in one of the film's actors—Gemma Clark, who played the daughter of Jeremy Irons' and Miranda Richardson's characters—contacting me and establishing a brief e-mail friendship.

"I Wasn't Always Like This"—The famous quote by Virginia Woolf is: "A woman must have money and a room of her own if she is to write fiction." *A Room of One's Own* (first published in October 1929 by the Hogarth Press in England, and by Harcourt Brace & Co. in the United States) relies heavily on an essay Woolf published in March 1929 in *Forum* as "Women and Fiction." Prior to publication, *A Room of One's Own* was delivered in a series of lectures at Cambridge University in October 1928. The Mary J. Blige quote is from her song "No More Drama" on the 2001 album of the same name.

"A Tale of Two Gardens"—The italicized quotations are from *A Tale of Two Cities*, by Charles Dickens, published in 1859. "It was the best of times, it was the worst of times, it was the age of wisdom, it was the age of foolishness, it was the epoch of belief, it was the epoch of incredulity, it was the season of Light, it was the season of Darkness, it was the spring of hope, it was the winter of despair, we had everything before us, we had nothing before us, we were all going direct to Heaven, we were all going direct the other way..."

"Almost Eve" — The children's text referred to, *I am a Bunny*, is by Ole Risom, with illustrations by Richard Scarry. It was published in 1963.

"Haleakala Sunrise" — The Mark Twain quote is from his semi-autobiographical book *Roughing It* (1872). The quote is oft-repeated in online promotional sites, including http://mauiguidebook.com/memorable-things-to-do-on-maui-11-20/. Annie Dillard's essay "Total Eclipse" is in *Teaching A Stone To Talk (1982)*. "Total Eclipse" was originally published in the Spring/Summer 1982 issue of *Anteaus*, the literary journal that was the first venture of Ecco press, which also publishes literary fiction and poetry. Drue Heinz, philanthropist, widow of H.G. "Jack" Heinz II (Heinz Company; iconic Ketchup and more), and publisher of *The Paris Review*, served as publisher of the magazine. Drue Heinz owns Hawthornden Castle. I met Drue Heinz when I received a Fellowship to attend the month-long Hawthornden Castle writers' retreat in 2004—she visited while I was there. She walked into the drawing room where the four other writers and I were seated, and immediately asked: "Who is the poet?" I meekly raised my hand.

"Plenty of Fish" — Names and details have been changed. The Canada Council for the Arts generously awarded funding for my short-fiction manuscript *Plenty of Fish*. I have lifted the title piece for use in this essay collection, because let's be honest here: some stories don't venture far from the truth.

"Back to the Garden"—The quote about the earliest gardens within a religious context is from *The Medicinal Garden: How to Grow and Use Your Own Medicinal Herbs* (Anne McIntyre, Henry Holt and Company, 1997). In my efforts to substantiate Luther's quote about gardening, I found this: "Even if I knew that tomorrow the world would go to pieces, I would still plant my apple tree."—Martin Luther (https://www.goodreads.com/author/quotes/29874.Martin_Luther)

"*Egészegédre*"—The Hungarian and I got our hundred days together, but not many more. The Biblical quote derives from Eccelsiastes1:9. "What has been is what will be and what has been done is what will be done; there is nothing new under the sun."

ACKNOWLEDGEMENTS

Thank you to the editors of these publications in which earlier versions of the following essays first appeared:

"Back to the Garden" (with photos) in *The Western Producer* as "Bond with friend grows with stroll through her garden" (2013)

"A Tale of Two Gardens" in *Transition Magazine* (2013)

"Blue Hawaii" in *Transition Magazine* (2011)

"Almost Eve" in *Transition Magazine* (2011)

"In the Field" (with photos) in *Hearts of the Country* as "In the Field: A Saskatchewan writer puts down the pen and picks up the crop" (2010) and in *The Western Producer* as "Harvest is a kind of poetry" (2009)

"Once Upon a Time in Bali" in *DiversitAS* (2009) as "Once Upon a Time in Bali: Adventures on a Mother-Son Vacation" (with photos)

"I Wasn't Always Like This" in *Transition Magazine* (2009)

"Road Trip" in *Country Roads: Memoirs from Rural Canada* (Nimbus Publishing, 2009) and *NeWest Review* (1996) as "Road Trip: Why I Write About Saskatchewan"

"Calle 55: Notes from an Exchange" in *Outside of Ordinary: Women's Travel Stories* (Second Story Press, 2005) as "Calle 55: Notes From the Canada-Mexico Writing/Photography Exchange"

A portion of "No Ocean, No Mountains: There's No Place Like Home," appeared (with photos) in the *See Scenic Saskatchewan* supplement to the *Western Producer* (2000). A version also aired on CBC Radio (SK) as "No Place Like Home" (2000)

The following essays were recognized with awards in Saskatchewan Writers' Guild Literary Competitions: "Blue Hawaii" (Second Place, 2009); "San Francisco: Photos Not Taken" (First Place, 2006); "I Wasn't Always Like This" (Honourable Mention, 2006); "Almost Eve" (Third Place, 2005)

ABOUT THE AUTHOR

Shelley A. Leedahl writes poetry, short fiction, novels, children's literature, and non-fiction. In addition to her eleven published books, her work appears in wide-ranging anthologies, including *The Best Canadian Poetry in English, 2013; I Found It at the Movies: An Anthology of Film Poems; Great Canadian Murder and Mystery Stories; Slice Me Some Truth: An Anthology of Canadian Creative Nonfiction; Country Roads: Memoirs from Rural Canada*; and *Outside of Ordinary: Women's Travel Stories*. She has received fellowships to attend artist retreats in Canada, the United States, and Europe. Aside from literary writing, she also works as a freelancer, editor, and writing instructor, and frequently presents in schools and libraries.

Leedahl was born in Kyle, Saskatchewan and has lived in numerous small Saskatchewan towns and Saskatoon, Calgary, Medicine Hat, Sechelt, and Edmonton. She now lives in Ladysmith, British Columbia.

Other Books by Shelley A. Leedahl

Fiction

Listen, Honey
Orchestra of the Lost Steps
Tell Me Everything
Sky Kickers

Poetry

Wretched Beast
The House of the Easily Amused
Talking Down The Northern Lights
A Few Words For January

Children & Juvenile

Riding Planet Earth
The Bone Talker

Eco-Audit
Printing this book using Rolland Enviro 100 Book
instead of virgin fibres paper saved the following resources:

Trees	Solid Waste	Water	Air Emissions
3	127 kg	10,398 L	418 kg